FRANK LEWINS

AUSTRALIAN
NATIONAL
UNIVERSITY

SOCIAL SCIENCE METHODOLOGY

A BRIEF
BUT CRITICAL
INTRODUCTION

M

First published 1992 by
MACMILLAN EDUCATION AUSTRALIA PTY LTD
107 Moray Street, South Melbourne 3205
6 Clarke Street, Crows Nest 2065

Associated companies and representatives
throughout the world

National Library of Australia
cataloguing in publication data

Lewins, Frank W. (Frank William).
 Social science methodology.

 Bibliography.
 ISBN 0 7329 1332 2.
 ISBN 0 7329 1331 4 (pbk.).

 1. Social sciences — Methodology. I. Title.

300.1

Set in Plantin and Frutiger
by Superskill Graphics, Singapore
Printed in Hong Kong

Contents

Preface

For some years now I have seen the need for an introduction to the basic principles of social science **methodology**. Although it is written with a sociologist's bias, most of the material in this book has application in all social sciences and, arguably, has something to say to beginners in all sciences. By 'methodology' I mean the systematic scrutiny of what researchers do and why they do it. This involves looking at areas such as the notion of **theory**, the relation between theory and evidence, the strengths and weaknesses of particular methods and, generally, understanding the nature of **analysis**.

Students may recognise some overlap between this book and parts of an earlier work I wrote on thesis writing (Lewins 1988). In the latter I argued that much of the skill in writing a thesis stems from understanding the basic methodological areas mentioned above. Also, I made explicit my own conception of science, which involved discussing issues such as the tension between '**the scientific method**' and the actual practice of science, and the role of **theory dependence**. Where there is overlap, I have attempted to recast the material to serve the different aim of understanding the nature of the practice of social science.

The need for a basic introduction to social science methodology arises for several reasons. First, there are several good books which cover the main territory of methodology but, unfortunately, are too advanced for the beginner. Second, the very nature of teaching social science in many tertiary institutions prevents a clear grasp of the fundamentals of methodology. Most obvious is the practice of teaching theory and methods separately, which has the effect of students not understanding the nature of the bridge between them. Finally, and perhaps most important, beginners in disciplines within the social sciences often already understand the fundamental principles of methodology as a result of their own life experiences but do not realise it. This is evident, for instance, in the day-to-day understanding most people have of the practice of medicine and law. Methodological questions, such as 'what is a theory?', 'are there degrees of **explanation**?', and 'what is the difference between theory testing and theory construction research?' may sound imposing in social science circles but are all understood and taken for granted in the common sense understanding of the doctor's consulting room and the courtroom. Compare, for instance, two common statements from medical practitioners:

'I think the patient has hepatitis but I will need to do some tests to confirm it.'

and

'I think we will need to do some tests to see if we can establish why the patient is ill.'

The first illustrates a doctor's initial assumption that the probable explanation of the patient's condition is hepatitis. Put differently, the starting point is a theory about why the patient is ill which, in turn, guides the choice of the evidence needed to confirm it. The second statement illustrates the arrival at a theory or diagnosis after evidence is at hand. In the general area of law, note the same difference between the statement in the courtroom:

'. . . the prosecution argues that the accused committed the crime and we will produce evidence to support that claim.'

and the implicit question posed by the police at an earlier stage in the case:

'who committed this crime?'

Theory is important in both types of statement. In the first it is tested; in the second it is constructed.

Without going into details at this point, all these statements are easily understood and, more to the point, the differences between each pair would be seen by most observers to be perfectly straightforward. Such statements are analogous to key principles in the practice of social science and all sciences and, hopefully, their selective use throughout this book will assist students to recognise the simplicity and everyday examples of many of the principles of methodology.

Finally, consistent with the notion of 'basic introduction', three features of this book are intended to serve that purpose. First, the message has been kept as brief as possible although it attempts to cover essential territory for students' first intellectual excursion into methodology. Second, the first mention of important terms are in bold type throughout the text and are defined and annotated in the glossary. Finally, footnotes and referencing have been kept to a minimum simply because, as a first text in methodology, it acknowledges that students will necessarily move to more advanced works, such as Rose's *Deciphering Sociological Research* (1982). I have found this book to be of great value and much of my own commitment to the study of methodology springs from working with its author.

Frank Lewins
Canberra

1
The Nature of Social Science

What is the nature of social science?

In my own discipline, students are often confronted in their first class of introductory sociology with the question 'what is sociology?' or 'what is it to be sociological?' What might seem straightforward to the experienced practitioner is often a difficult question for beginners in the discipline. It is not all that clear, for example, how investigative journalism and sociology differ, especially when they address the same topic such as poverty, suicide or unemployment. It is important that, before students are expected to deal with more complex aspects of methodology such as **validity of indicators**, **operationalising concepts** and the nature of theory testing and theory construction, they approach the intellectual stepping stones in the right order by first having a clear answer to the question above.

What then is the nature of social science? On the assumption that the principles of methodology of all social sciences are sufficiently similar, let me again use sociology as a single social science to address this question. Consider the following four hypothetical statements regarding crime.

Statement 1
Recent increase in the number of murders, rapes and burglaries is no accident. One would have to be less than mentally competent to overlook the obvious causal link between admitting waves of undesirables into this country and this new wave of extremist crime. Unless we return to the type of population we had in the past, how can we expect to rid

ourselves of this insidious form of crime which we have not seen before?

Statement 2
Recent evidence of an increase in the number of convictions for the serious crimes of murder, rape and armed robbery (Smith 1988) does not mean that there has been an increase in the number of those crimes. It is well documented that crime waves occur when police control is stepped up (Brown 1985, Black 1988). That is to say, when police, for whatever reason, have a 'crackdown' on crime, there are more arrests and subsequent convictions, which appears to the public as an increase in crime. This is a public perception that does not fit the available evidence. Research in three major cities shows that, despite fluctuations in the number of convictions for serious crime, the actual rate of those crimes (taking into account population increases) has remained stable (Pink 1987, Green 1988, White 1989). Hence, we can fruitfully examine crime in terms of 'control waves' rather than 'crime waves'.

Statement 3
The Minister for Law and Order said today that recent increase in crime in this country was the most serious social problem we have faced this century. She added that crime was primarily a result of the loss of the beneficial socialising effects of the family, a problem which was being addressed by the government's family policies. She explained that those policies included strategies to prevent divorce, which was the most destructive influence on children's lives and a cause of their turning to crime in adult life.

Statement 4
In the metropolitan area of Greytown in 1988 there were 50 murders, 200 rapes, 600 burglaries and 750 car thefts. The figures for Blacktown were identical except for the number of murders, where there were 61. In each city, 75% of each category of crime resulted in a charge being laid. Of those, 85% were convicted.

It would not give anything away to say that statement 2 'looks' sociological and statement 3 is journalistic in its orientation. But the important questions are:

(a) why should statements 2 and 3 be viewed this way?
(b) what sort of statements are 1 and 4?
(c) what are the similarities and differences between these statements?

Let us consider each question starting with (c). One obvious similarity is that all statements are about crime. Less obvious is the causal component in the first three statements; that is, they are suggesting that something is causing something else. In the first, it is the admission of waves of 'undesirables' which are said to cause the increase in serious crime. It is 'control waves' which cause the public perception of 'crime waves' in the second, and in the third it is the absence of effective socialisation and family breakdown which leads to crime. The differences, however, are more numerous. Statements 1 and 3 present no evidence in contrast to 2 and 4. Also, the first statement is explicitly emotional and prejudiced; the second introduces unfamiliar terms, such as 'control waves'; the third is describing what somebody else said; and the last one is reporting what appear to be straightforward occurrences. Of course, there are more differences, and possibly more similarities, but for our purposes recognition of this short list is sufficient. If these similarities and differences are fairly clear to the reader, then the first step in our understanding of methodology is successful.

The next step is to address question (b) and to identify what sort of statements we are dealing with. We have already noted that statement 2 'looks sociological' and that 3 is 'journalistic in orientation', but what about statements 1 and 4? It is not unreasonable to suggest that the first is a statement of prejudice and that the fourth is 'just facts'. So far, therefore, we have four types of statement to which we can assign the following labels:

1) prejudice
2) sociology

3) journalism
4) facts

In turning to the final question concerning why we view certain statements as 'sociological' and 'journalistic', we should also include 'prejudice' and 'facts'. Why do we put the above statements into these sorts of categories?

The similarities and differences identified earlier provide the key to answering this question. We noted that the first three had a causal component. That is, in attempting to show why crime had increased, they were offering an explanation, which is another way of saying that each was putting forward a theory concerning the increase in crime. But we also noted that statements 2 and 4 were the only ones that provided evidence. When we consider both the presence of a theory *and* the existence of evidence, we are close to understanding what sets sociology aside from the other types of statements. Figure 1.1 tells us that statements 1 and 3 have high explanatory capacity but lack evidence. Statement 4 contains evi-

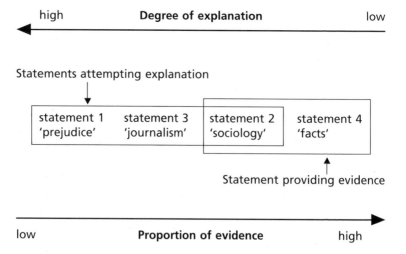

Figure 1.1 *The relation between explanation and evidence in sociology and other types of statement*

dence but lacks explanatory content in that it says nothing about *why* the apparent increase in crime has occurred. Statement 2, which to now we have labelled 'sociological' without saying why, is the only one which *attempts to provide an explanation which is based on the systematic use of evidence.* It is this quality of statement 2 which makes it sociological or, more broadly, a statement of social science. Explanation alone does not make a statement sociological, as statements 1 and 3 indicate. The important point to stress is that while a statement may have high explanatory value, it does not follow that it is supported by adequate evidence, nor that it is true. To draw on the medical analogy, statements such as 'All human illness is the will of God' have considerable explanatory content but, as sociologists (or as practitioners of any discipline for that matter) we cannot produce evidence to support them. In fact, in many cases like statement 1, it is the obvious disregard of evidence which enables the production of a strong explanation.

In short, social science is the attempt to explain social phenomena within the limits of available evidence. Admittedly, there are apparent 'grey' areas where, for example, investigative journalism has an explanatory dimension, and where prejudiced individuals present some evidence to support their dogmatic stances. However, in general the broad picture described above holds because the journalist is generally more interested in seeking a newsworthy story, and the bigot in selecting evidence which supports bigotry. Neither is committed to finding the best explanation of events surrounding them.

Having established that social science is concerned with finding explanations or theories of the social world within the limits of evidence, it is worth asking the question 'how and why do explanations come into existence?' To some extent we take this question for granted in that we rarely reflect on it. Explanations advanced by the defence and prosecution in the courtroom for the actions of the accused, or a doctor seeking a diagnosis after many medical tests on a seriously ill patient, are obvious instances where there is a *need* to produce an explanation. But what about the explanations offered in marine biology for the strange metabolism of sea sponges, or the explanation of bone and teeth development of prehistoric animals? The absence of an obvious need for explanation of those events prompts a closer look at the nature of scientific activity itself.

The nature of scientific activity

Many texts attempt to account for the nature of scientific activity by engaging in detailed discussions of 'the scientific method'. Apart from their often too technical approach, especially for new students in a discipline, it is really a case of the texts not answering the right question. Describing the scientific method is an answer to the question 'how does science proceed?' I say '*an* answer' rather than '*the* answer' because the scientific method is not the full story, as we shall discover. The question 'what is the nature of science?' or 'what is it to be scientific?' is really the place to begin.

No doubt there are many answers to this question within a variety of disciplines, with some practitioners arguing that certain answers were 'not science' or 'less scientific'. This sort of bickering often misses the point by focussing on method rather than the underlying principles which guide activity in a discipline. It is these underlying principles which are important because they are common to all disciplines and also because they help us understand why apparently useless explanations are sought after. There are five such principles:

1. To be scientific is to ask questions of the events covered by a particular discipline. These questions generally take the form of research. In the medical arena, for example, doctors may ask 'why is the incidence of cancer higher in this city compared to the rest of the country?' Such a question is a puzzle to be solved and this is often the main driving element in scientific discovery.

2. To be scientific is to accept that no aspect of the events being studied is immune from questioning; there are no 'sacred cows' in science. Remember, this claim is a statement of principle, which means that in practice we do avoid certain research questions. Sometimes we are not conscious of doing so because the questions are not even imaginable within a particular discipline. There were no medieval bacteriologists because questions about disease were largely theological questions. The question 'might there be an explanation of the plague which is non theological?' was for centuries not asked. To have posed such a question would have challenged the church's monopoly on the production and maintenance of 'correct' social knowledge.

On the other hand, some research questions are consciously avoided for ideological, psychological and/or professional reasons. A researcher whose lifetime has been devoted to formulating and defending a particular explanation or theory, for example, would have great difficulty, if not reluctance, in openly asking the question 'is my theory correct?'.

3. To be scientific is to attempt to answer research questions with **empirical** evidence. Such answers are often theories or explanations. The answer to the medical researcher's question about the incidence of cancer in a particular city may be based on the notion of carcinogenic substances in a highly polluted atmosphere — something we hear a lot about today, but an explanation which was not so taken for granted several decades ago.

4. To be scientific is to accept that theories are always, at best, tentatively true. There is no absolute truth in scientific activity, no absolute certainty. This is evident in all disciplines for, although some researchers hold onto their 'pet' theories in the face of counter evidence, we see numerous examples of 'spent' theories. The alcoholic-as-criminal is an explanation no longer heard in the courtroom. It is largely taken for granted that alcoholism is now a medical problem. And today, of course, few if any scholars would accept that plague can be explained by the will of God.

5. To be scientific is to accept that the practice of asking questions builds on previous research or answers to other questions, and is therefore capable of contributing to an accumulation of what we call scientific knowledge.

An important point which springs from this discussion is that scientific discovery can only come about if we ask the 'right' questions. The necessity of asking the right questions is something which occurs in many other areas of life and, because this is so often taken for granted, needs some clarification. The point should be obvious in a couple of examples. Take the situation of the medieval sailors. No doubt they asked or wondered many times 'if we sail too far from land, will we fall off the edge of the earth?' This sort of question was not the 'right' question to yield new knowledge because it implicitly assumed that the earth was flat and, therefore, that the answer was 'yes'. By contrast, a different intellectual mood hangs over a completely different question. Imagine the same medieval sailors asking 'why is it that a ship appears to sink as well as get smaller as it sails into the distance?' It does not take much imagination to see that this question can lead to discovery, possibly by it leading to another question, such as 'is the earth really flat?' This situation and many others reveal barriers to asking the right questions, something we will address when we discuss theory dependence.

In summary, we can say that scientific discovery comes about as a result of systematic curiosity; 'systematic' indicating that asking questions does not take place in a haphazard fashion but in accord with principles 2 to 5. As we will see, some scientists are more curious than others, being less influenced by assumptions which prevent the right questions being asked. Research being influenced by certain assumptions opens up the issue of theory dependence, which deserves a lengthy comment. This discussion is necessarily more intellectually involved than other parts of this book and, therefore, can be treated as background material by the introductory student.

Theory dependence

'**Theory dependence**' is a somewhat imprecise term which refers to the influence of certain, often unstated, assumptions of the research process. 'Theory' points to the implicit and broad explanatory character of researchers' assumptions, while 'dependence' indicates that the nature of a given area of the research process is dependent on those assumptions.

To accept the theory dependent nature of research means that it is axiomatic that notions such as 'objectivity' and 'value freedom' are not guaranteed by 'the scientific method' — the strategy of research which has been associated with immunity from 'subjectivity' and researchers' 'values'. Although general scholarly interest in the contingent nature of research is, arguably, a legacy of Marx's analysis of ideology and materialist view (specifically of history), the independence of research from researchers' unstated and unrecognised assumptions has been systematically challenged by a variety of scholars. Popper (1968, 1972), Feyerabend (1975) and Kuhn (1970) illuminate the claim that observations in all research are theory dependent or contingent on researchers' own theoretical maps of the world. The Marxist scholar, Ollman, makes a similar point about contingency in the choice of a research topic and its **conceptual framework**. In discussing the significance of the term 'abstracts', that is, 'where and how one draws boundaries and establishes units . . . in which to think about the world', he notes that

The assumption is that while the qualities we perceive with our five senses actually exist as parts of nature, the conceptual distinctions that tell us where one thing ends and the next one begins both in space and across time are social and mental constructs. However great the influence of what the world is on how we draw these boundaries, it is ultimately we who draw the boundaries, and people coming from different cultures and from different philosophical traditions can and do draw them differently (1986: xiii).

In the l970s, social scientists witnessed a flurry of activity on this intellectual front with the appearance of works such as those from Willers (1971, 1973) and Hirst (1975, 1976). Although these works and those mentioned above are by no means exhaustive, they illustrate two key points. First, not all areas of research influenced by researchers' assumptions are given equal scrutiny by scholars. Theory dependent observation, including the problem of induction, is, as Ollman reminds us, prominent ahead of the contingent nature of the choice of a research topic. However, some areas are barely examined at all and I shall return to these later. Second, there is no scholarly work which deals with all areas of theory dependence under the one heading.

If all scholars were convinced of the contingent nature of the research process, then this discussion would not be necessary. However, it appears that in scholarly circles Hempel's (1966:11) notion of 'ideal scientific inquiry' still exists.[1] Even as recently as the early 1980s, Chalmers was able to speak of 'self avowed "scientists" ' in American colleges and universities pursuing 'the empirical method', which consists of

> . . . the collection of 'facts' by means of careful observation and the subsequent derivation of laws and theories from those facts by some kind of logical procedure (1982: xvi).

Chalmers' stressing of 'empirical' and 'facts' is a criticism of scholars' uncritical acceptance of the proposition that the scientific method is independent of researchers' assumptions.

The purpose then of this discussion is to identify all areas of theory dependence in the research process. Locating these areas is important, not only because it brings them together under one heading and identifies the full extent of theory dependence in all research, but also because of the central importance of theory dependence in the intellectual development of all disciplines. It is especially important for social science because it illuminates the extent of social influences on the production of knowledge.

In light of the above, it is not surprising that the major problem with the scientific method is that it is not an accurate representation of how research actually proceeds. Inaccuracy stems largely from failure to recognise and acknowledge the role of theory dependence throughout the research process. Such failure is evident, for example, in the matter of fact way scholars are told that their treatment of data 'has to be objective and unbiased' (Rummel 1964: 269). Before turning to the specific instances of theory dependence, it needs to be said that bias is not a uniform quality of research and not all forms of bias are necessarily undesirable. The latter proposal applies to theory dependence and needs to be distinguished from that bias which produces deception, distortion or grossly unreasonable conclusions.

Turning to the first area of theory dependence, it is obvious that there is a form of bias evident in the choice of an acceptable research topic in a given discipline. What counts as an acceptable research question in any discipline is shaped by unstated and often unrecognised assumptions governing the nature and limits of that discipline. This is implicit in retorts such as 'that's not chemistry !' or 'that's good medicine !'. Illustrating this a little further, it is obvious that the research topics listed below fall within the corresponding disciplines and, therefore, are acceptable as physics, sociology and so on (cf Almack 1930: 37).

Research topic	*Discipline*
What is the torsional stress distribution in prismatic bars?	Physics
What are the social causes of divorce?	Sociology
What are the effects of the Botulinus bacillus on human physiology?	Medicine
What is the size of the sugar market in the USA?	Economics

In choosing these particular topics, scholars are biased to the extent that they are influenced by unstated assumptions surrounding the theoretical territory of their discipline. This is an acceptable and unavoidable form of bias and is illuminated by turning to the second area of theory dependence — the choice of a worthwhile topic.

Worthwhile research is best illustrated by pointing to those topics which all researchers know to be unworthwhile. One only has to compare the topics listed above with the following:

Research topic	*Discipline*
What is the torsional stress distribution in chocolate bars?	Physics
What is the relationship between the size of Christmas cards and the social attributes of their senders?	Sociology
What is the mean size of the adolescent pimple?	Medicine
What is the extent of wealth in wishing wells?	Economics

What is important about these examples of unworthwhile research is that each is technically an acceptable topic in its own discipline. That is, if one wanted, for example, to study torsional stress in chocolate bars, then it would be a question to be explored with the concepts of physics and not medicine. One could say, of course, that these trivial topics could become worthwhile if circumstances changed. Some might argue, for instance, that previously trivial research on atomic particles became worthwhile once the military implications of splitting the atom were recognised. However, the point is that when this sort of transition does occur, it does so because of factors outside the discipline concerned, which reinforces the theory dependent nature of the situation. Put differently, the newly discovered worth of such topics is contingent on what are often unstated assumptions which, in turn, are shaped by social and historical circumstances.

Another aspect of theory dependence concerns the choice of a particular research topic. This was foreshadowed above when looking at Ollman's notion of 'abstracts' and is a particularly important area of theory dependence because it is perhaps the most frequent and obvious in research. When we look at a range of research problems, we can infer not only the discipline but, in many cases, the particular theoretical assumptions of the researcher. One could, for example, be fairly confident of pinpointing the particular orientation of researchers asking the following questions:

Research topic	*Discipline*
Why has the revolution not occurred in Britain as Marx said it would?	Sociology
Keynesian economics: science or sham?	Economics
What is the extent of unacknowledged influence of high levels of air pollution in the causation of respiratory disease?	Medicine
The missing calculation: do bridges fall down because of the oversight of engineers?	Physics

Of course, these questions illustrate theory dependence in all three areas mentioned so far. Their formulation indicates the influence of the conceptual territory of each discipline so that they are recognisable as acceptable questions. They implicitly point to the audiences in each discipline which would defend these questions as worthwhile research; and they give a good indication of the type of orientation of the researcher asking the question.

By confining our attention to these three areas of theory dependence, not so hypothetical illustrations are evident in a number of areas. Jones, for example, illuminates what appears to have been, and possibly still is, a long running dispute in history circles over what sorts of things historians should study and, therefore, the sorts of questions which are acceptable and worthwhile. Pointing to tension on this issue in the mid-nineteenth century, Jones noted that:

> As late as 1925, H.W.C. Davis, Regius Professor at Oxford, attacked "those self-styled social historians" who "tell us that what we most need to know about any civilisation in the past is what its poorer and more illiterate members thought and did . . . our common humanity is best studied in the most eminent examples that it has produced of every type of human excellence" (1977: 98).

On a more general plane, Kuhn (1970) highlights this same theory dependence in his recognition of the propensity of scientific disciplines to adhere to 'paradigms' in which the everyday practice of 'normal science' consists of answering questions arising from within the paradigm. This 'mopping up' activity is another way of saying that adherence to a paradigm in a discipline influences both the choice of a particular topic and its worth.

Theory dependence surfaces not only in the areas mentioned above, but also in the process of certain research questions not being asked. In any society there are beliefs and ways of seeing the world which are so embedded that they prevent its scholars from seriously asking questions of a contrary nature. Such a closed situation often extends beyond the scientific community and it is often as members of a particular society and not as scientists that researchers avoid certain questions. In social science circles in industrialised countries for example, the notion of economic reward for human endeavour is so ingrained that an alternative is not generally imagined, and certainly does not influence the sorts of research questions which scholars ask. It is because such attitudes exist that theories which challenge 'paradigms' receive such a hostile reception; that is, until a scientific revolution occurs in a paradigm shift. Lister's 'germ' theory of disease is a good illustration of what was once seen as an outrageous explanation of sepsis. It was outrageous because, up until the 'revolution' in Victorian medicine which accepted Lister's contribution, questions about patients' well being were confined to the taken for granted assumptions of the day which did not include concepts such as 'germs'. As Lister himself said in 1883:

> Nowadays antiseptic treatment is not a very complicated business, either in theory or in practice . . . [however] there was a time when such remarks might have met with a very different reception (quoted in Youngson 1979: 152–54)[2].

A related but more familiar domain of theory dependence occurs in the process of selecting evidence to answer a research question. This process is often referred to as theory laden or theory dependent observation. Within any disciplinary framework, and in light of the particular theory or concepts in the intellectual foreground, it is not the case that all events are capable of being perceived and selected as evidence. Events are evidence to the extent that they are selected as such, and this depends on assumptions about what the events are evidence for. Before observers imagined plague was transmitted by rats, they did not perceive rat infestations as evidence. Youngson makes a similar point concerning Lister's work:

> This ['germ' theory of infection] was an achievement of theory . . . the information on which the deduction was based was readily available . . . if other men in the mid 1860s took the hint, none of them can have understood the medical implications in the complete way that Lister did (Youngson 1979: 154–55).

Philosophers often discuss this type of theory dependence under sub headings such as 'Observation statements presuppose theory' and 'Observation and experiment are guided by theory' and in doing so draw on the previously mentioned work of Popper, Feyerabend and Kuhn (e.g. see Chalmers 1982: 22–37). Before turning to the final area for discussion, it is necessary to elaborate another aspect of theory dependent observation which is generally referred to as the problem of induction.

The problem of induction centres around formulating general principles from information about discrete events; that is, moving from the particular to the general. Without entering into the philosophical arguments about this problem (see Chalmers 1982: 13–21; Hempel 1966: 10ff.), it is enough to note that many philosophers claim that there is no such thing as induction, or that there is an extremely limited sense in which the term can be used. The critique of induction, for our purposes, rests on the claim that it is really based on hidden deductive premises. Suppose, for example, that as a researcher you were asked to observe pedestrians' characteristics by standing on a street corner at lunch time with the aim of arriving at some generalisations through the process of induction. Also suppose that, as you began your observation, the entire staff of a large department store staged a mass walkout. Now here is the point: if those individuals constituted the bulk of your observations, you would realise that in attempting to arrive at general statements of pedestrians' characteristics, factors such as height, weight and hair colour might be valid in the so-called process of induction, but factors such as the wearing of coloured uniforms with a department store logo would be invalid. The latter obviously would be invalid because of your prior knowledge of the generalisation that not all pedestrians wear distinctive, coloured uniforms.

The sixth area of theory dependence is best described as *ad hoc* modification, a term which Chalmers uses in his wider discussion of falsificationism (1982: 38–76). As the term suggests, *ad hoc* modification involves altering the findings of any piece of research so that they conform to certain theoreti-

cal maps in that discipline. Without opening up the philosophical complexities of this area, an illustration of *ad hoc*
modification provided by Chalmers will make the point :

> Having carefully observed the moon through his newly in-
> vented telescope, Galileo was able to report that the moon
> was not a smooth sphere but that its surface abounded in
> mountains and craters. His Aristotelian adversary had to
> admit that things did appear that way when he repeated the
> observations for himself. But the observations threatened a
> notion fundamental for many Aristotelians, namely, that all
> celestial bodies are perfect spheres. Galileo's rival defended
> his theory in the face of the apparent falsification in a way that
> was blatantly ad hoc. He suggested that there was an invisible
> substance on the moon, filling the craters and covering the
> mountains in such a way that the moon's shape was perfectly
> spherical. When Galileo inquired how the presence of the
> invisible substance might be detected, the reply was that there
> was no way in which it could be detected (1982: 52).

Recognition of these six areas of theory dependence is important because, among other things, it represents a range of
gaps in the scientific method or, to be more precise, the
so called 'ideal scientific' method (Hempel 1966: 11). Few
accounts of the scientific method ever hint at more than one
or two areas of theory dependence. These gaps are evident in
Figure 1.2, which incorporates the six areas covered above.

Even if one accepted that not all but some areas of theory
dependence apply to research activity, then narrow accounts
of the scientific method would still be inaccurate. The extent
to which scholars still operate within such a narrow account
of the scientific method, by their uncritical acceptance of the
non-contingent nature of the research process, is a measure
of the gap in their understanding and their not having a
realistic account of the research process. Accordingly, it needs
to be stressed that identifying areas of theory dependence is
not necessarily a criticism of research. If there is any problem

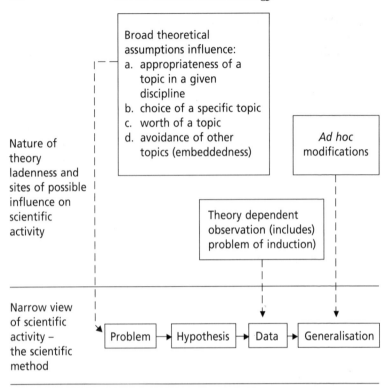

Figure 1.2   *The research process incorporating areas of theory dependence*

associated with theory dependence in principle, it lies in not recognising and/or refusing to accept its existence.

In conclusion, this discussion of key areas of theory dependence which impinge on the research process has been a 'geographical' statement rather than a philosophical exercise. It has aimed to highlight the location rather than philosophical principles of theory dependence. This sort of exposition is particularly important for social scientists because, although I dispute the claim that the social sciences are in principle not like the other sciences, the extent of theory dependence in some social sciences is likely to be more extensive than in other disciplines. This is simply because those scientists are often more immersed in their own subject matter.

Having examined the more realistic picture of the practice of science in general and social science in particular, it is important now to look more closely at the sorts of answers to scientists' research questions; that is, to scrutinise the area we refer to as 'theory' or 'explanation'.

Degrees of explanation

When earlier discussing sociology in relation to 'journalism', 'facts', and 'prejudice', we saw that there are degrees of explanation. An explanation attempts to account for the existence of a given realm of events so that having an explanation enables one to see *why* and/or *how* and/or *what* events are related, follow on from each other, and can be predicted and/or changed. From this definition it is clear why theory and explanation are synonymous. We saw that the statements above, notwithstanding whether they were true or not, contained explanations or theories with a high explanatory content which were able to account for why certain events occurred. In other words, they were able to provide a more complete answer to a *why* question. Causal theories have the highest explanatory content because, in being able to locate the causes of a particular event, they provide the conditions under which it does or does not exist. This in turn enables prediction and, in some cases, actual intervention to change outcomes. Knowing, for example, the cause of a particular disease enables doctors to control its course by intervening with drugs or surgery.

Answers to such 'why' questions are explanations, but not all explanations are answers to 'why' questions. This is so for at least two reasons. First, we do not always have sufficient access to evidence to answer such questions. In the medical arena, for example, 'why do we go to sleep?' is a worthwhile question and difficult to answer because of the lack of good evidence. Second, we do not always need answers to 'why' questions but, rather, answers to 'what' and 'how' questions.

For example, in attempting to arrive at an explanation for a crime, it is often more important to know what the accused did and how he/she did it than to know why. Similarly, in the medical context, it is often more important for the purposes at hand to know, for example, how malaria is transmitted, how the liver manufactures bile, and what the signs and symptoms of a particular disease are, than to have answers to 'why' questions. Incidentally, it is worth noting that in the first instance the 'how' question is virtually the same as the 'why' version in that asking why malaria is transmitted is really to ask how. This situation is not always the case, for in the second example the question as to why the liver manufactures bile cannot be answered within medicine because of its somewhat theological (or ontological) nature.

The social sciences have theories with more or less explanatory power because of the impossibility, the difficulty, or their being no need to address 'why' questions. In other words, we often have less than a causal explanation of social phenomena because it is too difficult or there is no way to assemble the evidence needed to mount a causal argument (see below). Or we may simply prefer to explore another level of explanation. It is this range of levels of explanation which now needs more scrutiny.

There are at least five identifiable levels of explanation in social science. At the most explanatory level is the causal theory, followed by laws, models, taxonomies, and descriptions:

Causal theory is the most explanatory, as we have seen, because it generally provides the most complete answer to a 'why' question and, in doing so, posits the conditions under which the events being explained happen. This is shown by the comparison of levels of explanation in social science, medicine and law summarised in Figure 1.3. Starting with the question which has fascinated social scientists for over a century — 'why do suicide rates vary?' — and borrowing from Emile Durkheim, the somewhat hypothetical answer offered is a typical causal explanation (see Fig. 1.3). That it provides the most complete answer to the 'why' question is evident if we place the word 'because' immediately in front of the explanation, a claim that is more obvious when the other levels of explanation are treated in the same way.

Laws posit the recurring nature of particular relationships. A principal law of thermo dynamics, for example, which holds that heat cannot of itself pass from one body to a hotter body, claims that the observed relationship always follows a particular pattern without exception. But where is the explanation in a law? This is clearer if we return to the question 'why do suicide rates vary?' If we attempt to answer this question with a law, we see that by using the word 'because' in front again, the answer is useful but not as complete as the causal explanation. It is not as complete because it only tells you that where religious affiliation has a certain quality, suicide rates are low. It is not saying that religious affiliation has anything to do with the cause of suicide rates. It is merely saying that where you find one factor — strong religious affiliation — you find the other — lower suicide rates. This is a little like saying that where you find leaves falling off deciduous trees, you also find birds are migrating. In short, without having to open up the more subtle aspects of causal arguments which will follow shortly, the law is a less complete answer to the question and, hence, less explanatory.

Models are representations of something existing in the world. They do not exist themselves but, by their simplified nature, provide a clearer picture of the world. A basic illustration of a model is a street directory. It is obvious that particular streets and places do not exist as parallel lines and dots, but such a scale representation of the real world is explanatory to the extent that it becomes possible to answer questions such as 'where am I?' when one is lost. In social science research, models are used extensively. One type is the causal model, which is a representation of a broad array of processes operating in the social world. The hypothetical causal model offered in Figure 1.4 posits a relationship be-

Degree of explanation	SOCIOLOGY Q. Why do suicide rates vary?	MEDICINE Q. Why are some cancers more fatal than others?	LAW Q. Did the accused commit the murder?
Causal	The rate of suicide in all societies is principally influenced by the degree of individuals' social integration. Social integration is the nature of individuals' social connectedness, which provides feelings of belonging to a larger entity and acts as a shield against social isolation and the propensity to suicide.	The rate of onset of death from cancer depends on the type of malignancy involved. Type A cancers reach maturity quickly and then are capable of sending their invasive secondaries to other organs in the body. Type B cancers are slow to develop and therefore take longer to produce life threatening secondaries.	It is the contention of the prosecution that the explanation for the evidence before the court is that the accused murdered the deceased.
Law	Strong degrees of religious affiliation in any society are always accompanied by low suicide rates.	All type A cancers kill 90% of patients within 5 years of onset. All type B cancers kill 30% of patients in the same period.	It is a well known axiom that all murderers return to the scene of the crime and we know from witnesses that the accused was seen at the deceased's home on the night of the crime.
Model			

	social science	medicine	law
Taxonomy	Suicide rates are illuminated by three categories of moral sense: (i) over attachment to norms (altruism) (ii) under attachment to norms (anomie) (iii) no awareness of norms at all (non social)	Fatalities from cancer are partly explained by the categories of cancer, ie. fatal — malignant — type A fast growing (high risk) / type B slow growing (low risk); non fatal — benign — no risk	lover / spouse / parent / child / relative 66% — deranged 7% / professionals 8% / personal antagonists 10% / other 9%. Categories of those convicted of murder
Description	Suicide rates have increased in recent decades in western industrialised countries. The concern over this increase is matched by the difficulty of explaining this phenomenon. Of particular concern are the vulnerability of particular social categories, especially the unemployed; the young; married women; and unmarried men.	Death from cancer has increased in the 20th century, especially in western industrialised countries. Despite heavy research efforts and government policies aimed at prevention, little progress has been achieved in combating the death rate from a few types. The medical world is having a rethink on the worth of treatment, especially surgery, for those categories.	Murder rates are of concern because they are increasing. Both the number of individuals murdered and the number of convictions obtained in the last decade have increased by 100%. Surveys show that the public's concern is mainly based on fear for their own lives.

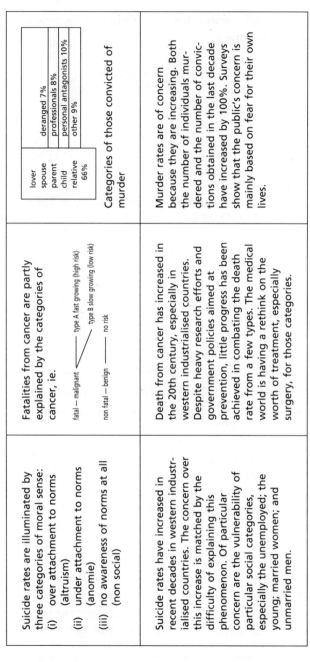

Figure 1.3 *Comparison of levels of explanation in social science, medicine and law*

tween individual's education, first job, father's job, mother's job, and current income.

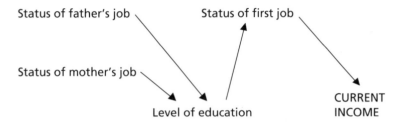

Figure 1.4 *Hypothetical causal model illustrating influences on current income*

It is a model because it is only a representation of the processes said to be operating in the social world. That is, it does not show 'how' or 'why' level of education, for example, exerts any influence on current income and, for this reason, is less explanatory than a causal theory. Looking more closely at a causal theory on the same subject, it would show how and why level of education is related to the attainment of educational qualifications in industrialised societies, which in turn is a major factor determining attainment of more highly rewarded jobs.

*Taxonomie*s are no more than classification schemes. The medical example in Figure 1.3 uses the classification of cancers into malignant and benign. We know that the use of this simple taxonomy does not explain a great deal about cancer by postulating causes but it is partly explanatory to the extent that it enables doctors to predict outcomes and to determine the best treatment and so on. We constantly use these taxonomies in our everyday life. It is not easy to say whether they are right or wrong simply because they are fashioned for the purposes at hand. When we do our laundry, we often classify clothes as 'very dirty', 'slightly soiled' and so on. But on other occasions, when we have other purposes, the categories could just as easily be 'coloureds' and 'whites'.

A very good illustration of these different purposes is evident in the way social scientists classify social phenomena. Take, for example, the following terms:

disabled person	heretic
jail	court marshalled soldier
priest	prisoner
religious training	military academy
prison warder	medical recovery
military training	military officer
doctor	prisoner rehabilitation
convent	hospital

Lists like this one often appear in intelligence tests where respondents are asked to categorise the items and then give their categories a heading. In these exercises the categories chosen are generally based on everyday experience. Such a categorisation of the list above might yield the following:

medically related	*prison related*
disabled person	jail
doctor	prison warder
medical recovery	prisoner
hospital	prisoner rehabilitation

religion related	*military related*
priest	military training
religious training	court marshalled soldier
heretic	military academy
convent	military officer

These categories seem to be a straightforward case of like being matched with like. However, to illustrate a completely different purpose, a social scientist might categorise this same list as follows:

socially defined deviants	*total institutions*
disabled person	jail
court marshalled soldier	convent
prisoner	military academy
heretic	hospital

social roles	*social processes*
priest	religious training
prison warder	military training
doctor	medical recovery
military officer	prisoner rehabilitation

This classification is neither better nor worse than the first. It simply serves a different purpose, that is to identify what goes with what in terms of the concepts social scientists are interested in — 'social roles', 'social processes' and so on. The explanatory value of this sort of taxonomy is that it helps us identify the similar properties of apparently diverse social situations, such as jails and convents.

Descriptions are accounts of events which adopt a particular standpoint, either consciously or unconsciously. When a doctor asks a medical student to describe a patient's condition, the student knows, and the doctor expects, that the description will be in terms relevant to the practice of medicine. It would be totally irrelevant if the student started describing aspects of the patient's jewellery or hair style. All scientific disciplines share this property which, alongside the discussion concerning theory dependence in science, demonstrates that there is no such thing as a completely unbiased description. This is simply because when we describe anything, whether it is for every day purposes or for scientific research, we describe it with the categories and concepts of our major preoccupation in mind. Not surprisingly, descriptions have the lowest level of explanatory value but it is evident that they do have explanatory value in that most descriptions quickly indicate the observer's discipline or starting point. This in turn limits the sort of evidence one can expect to analyse. A simple illustration of this hidden orientation in descriptions is to wonder how an automotive engineer, a traffic engineer and a psychologist would describe the same, serious motor car accident (see Brown 1963: 14–25).

Having claimed that a causal theory offers the greatest degree of explanation it is necessary to look more closely at what we mean by the notion of causality.

Causality

By identifying of levels of explanation, the question is raised as to why a researcher would ever bother to explain certain events with anything other than a causal explanation, given that this is the most explanatory domain of theory. Apart from those cases where a causal explanation is not the most appropriate explanation simply because of the question being asked, there are those situations where insufficient evidence does not allow a causal explanation, a point foreshadowed above. The obvious question to address at this point is 'what is the nature of evidence required for a causal theory?'

Before outlining the criteria of a causal argument two important points need to be discussed.

1. The notion of causality is not something which should be taken for granted (see Gibbs 1972: 20–27). In some scholarly circles the idea of one thing causing another is rejected completely and, for this reason, it is worth having some grasp of two prominent arguments against causality. There is the view that nothing worth explaining ever has a single cause but, rather, it is the product of a many factors or, as some texts put it, a part of a multi causal picture. The hypothetical causal models in Figures 1.3 and 1.4 are illustrations of this point. Discussion of events having many causes involves the use of terms such as 'necessary and sufficient conditions' to which we will turn in a moment. Another view holds that it makes little sense to focus on some small aspect of reality when we say that A causes B, or even when a variety of factors are said to cause B, because everything is a part of a complex causal chain in which things are caused and in turn cause other things. The true causal account would involve detailing every cause of every cause and so on.

In response to these arguments, most social scientists accept that social phenomena are involved in multi causal situations. If we took the problem of endless causal chains seriously, we would be involved in similarly endless theological arguments about the first cause of all things. Accepting the view that the social world involves multi causality, we should also freely admit that there are difficulties in arbitrarily focusing on a small part of reality. However, it is not practicable to do otherwise. The main point to realise is that the limited causal framework all scientists work with is for convenience, and is not a total statement of the situation under scrutiny. It is important to stress this realistic view of causality because it is not something we can do without. If doctors, for instance, were reduced to saying something like:

'I am not able to say whether your ill health has a cause, but I do know that you have a fifty per cent chance of surviving five years.'

they would find the practice of medicine impossible because it is only by having a causal theory of disease that doctors are able to intervene with treatment. In short, causality is explicit and implicit in the theories of all disciplines, which brings us to the second main point.

2. In social research one often finds causal explanations which do not use the word 'cause'. Instead we find a range of synonyms which are worth identifying. It is not so important to say why these synonyms are used but it is important to recognise them. The following list is not exhaustive but includes the terms frequently found in social science literature:

produces,
affects,
effects change,
leads to,
stimulates,
influences,
impinges on.

One cannot fully understand the idea of causality without an understanding of the terms 'necessary and sufficient conditions'. They are anything but technical, philosophical terms, for they frequently appear in the literature. Take, for example, the following hypothetical paragraph which one could imagine finding in a sociological account of suicide:

> Sociologists do not pretend to offer all the causes for variation in the rates of suicide in particular locations. Social integration is certainly not the necessary and sufficient condition which some researchers imagine. However, the degree of social integration would appear to be a necessary factor. Of course, there are other, perhaps undiscovered, factors which are also necessary conditions. We believe that social integration is a necessary condition because in all research on suicide we see two separate factors impinging on individuals' degree of social integration. Those factors are the level of connectedness to formal and informal networks and the quality of those connections.

To understand what is meant by necessary and sufficient conditions, it will be useful to translate this paragraph into another causal model, such as those used in Figures 1.3. and 1.4 (see Fig. 1.5).

From the text and the diagram, the meaning of 'necessary and sufficient conditions' becomes clearer. 'Necessary', as the name implies, means that a specific condition or factor is necessary for some event to occur. Without it the event cannot happen. What the causal model is saying is that a certain degree of social integration is necessary for a certain rate of suicide. However, it alone does not affect the rate of suicide; other factors also impinge on it. Put differently, degree of social integration is necessary but is not sufficient to change the suicide rate.

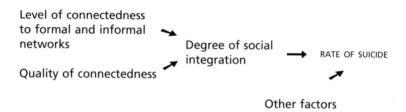

Level of connectedness
to formal and informal
networks

Degree of social
integration   RATE OF SUICIDE

Quality of connectedness

Other factors

Figure 1.5 *Hypothetical causal model illustrating influences on rate of suicide*

These terms are not complex and, therefore, need to be understood by the analyst of social research. Given we have already acknowledged that events rarely have one cause, it is worth thinking of actual examples to illustrate the four logically possible relationships between necessary and sufficient conditions. If, for example, we put forward a causal relationship between A and B, there are four possibilities:

1 A is both necessary and sufficient to cause B.

Some scholars claim that Weber held that the Protestant Ethic was the sole cause of the Spirit of Capitalism.

2 A is necessary but not sufficient to cause B.

Infection with the TB bacillus is required before one contracts the disease but it is not its only cause.

3 A is sufficient but not necessary to cause B.

Conviction for armed robbery will lead to a prison sentence but one can go to prison for other crimes.

| 4 | A is neither necessary nor sufficient to cause B. | Drinking milk leads to a healthy body! |

Returning to the criteria of a causal argument, what is the nature and extent of evidence one must have to be sure of demonstrating a causal relationship between two or more factors? The literature varies on this question (cf. Labovitz and Hagedorn 1971: 3ff. and Stinchcombe 1968: 32ff.) and also omits some essential points; hence, the following is an attempt at completeness. Five minimum criteria are required:

  1 *Covariation*   Put technically, this means there needs to be at least two values of the **independent variable** — or the factor thought to have an influence — and, similarly, at least two values of the **dependent variable** — or thing caused. If, for example, a sociologist wanted to see what factors might be influencing the high suicide rate in a particular town, it would be insufficient, knowing that there was a low degree of social integration in the town, to posit this as a cause. To satisfy the need for covariation, it would be necessary to have evidence of another town in which the suicide rate was low, and to have access to the nature of that town's degree of social integration. If the picture looked something like this:

| *Town A* | high degree of social integration | low rate of suicide |
| *Town B* | low degree of social integration | high rate of suicide |

then there would be two values of both the degree of social integration and the rate of suicide. However, although the minimum requirement would be met and notwithstanding the other criteria of a causal argument, it would not follow that a causal relationship existed. It could be pure chance that the pattern observed in the two towns is the way it is and that there is some other, unknown cause for the different suicide rates.

This point is perhaps more obvious when we look at a

doctor's reasoning when confronted with a patient who complains of severe abdominal pain and believes a serious disease to be the cause. The patient's logic might follow the same lines as the case above:

Normally	no pain	no serious disease
Lately	severe pain	serious disease

The doctor, however, while admitting that this reasoning may be correct, would no doubt caution the patient by stressing that there could be other causes of the pain.

In light of the role of unknown factors, ideally it is desirable to have many values of the variables thought to be causally related. When those values are quantifiable in uniform units, such as income in dollars or temperature in degrees centigrade, we are able to establish the degree of association between two variables. Hospitals, for example, know that as a result of years of experience, or having many values, there is a strong association between the nature of the weather, especially the temperature, and the number of motor car accidents per thousand population. Disregarding the possibility of changing rates of car ownership, the picture might be graphed as illustrated in Figure 1.6.

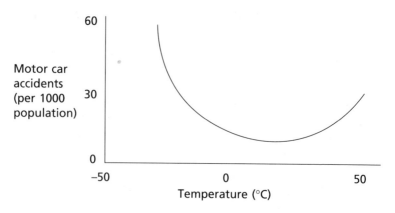

Figure 1.6 *Hypothetical association between temperature and rate of motor car accidents*

Such a picture tells us that there is a strong relationship or association between increasing temperatures in the summer or decreasing temperatures in the winter and the rate of motor car accidents, and would represent a strong case for believing a causal relationship existed between temperature and the rate of motor car accidents.

Of course, it needs to be stressed that having strong association does not necessarily entail a causal relationship. We acknowledge a strong association between the amount of leaves falling off deciduous trees and the number of birds migrating to warmer regions without imagining a causal connection. This is because we *know* of the existence of an independent factor — the onset of winter — which accounts for the association between the behaviour of birds and leaves.

This might sound obvious and trite but there are many situations in social research where that third and independent factor is not so obvious. In medical circles, the strong association between the number of cigarettes one smokes and the likelihood of contracting lung cancer is well known. In fact, the same association is accepted by the tobacco industry. The difference is that the former believe there is a causal relationship between smoking and lung cancer, whereas the latter does not. The tobacco industry often attempts to blame a third, independent factor which explains both the desire to smoke to excess and the vulnerability to lung cancer. This type of argument is closely bound to another criterion of a causal argument — establishing non-spuriousness — which is discussed later.

2 *Constancy of association*   This is the requirement that covariation or association remains constant over time. Using any of the examples mentioned so far, it is not difficult to see that spasmodic association or covariation undermines any assumption of a causal relationship. For example, if during the month of January in town B there was a strong association between individuals' low degree of social integration and their suicide, followed by no association whatsoever in February, then it would be precarious to propose causality. If a

similar on again–off again relationship existed between smoking and lung cancer, then we can be sure there would be far less certainty about the role of cigarette smoking.

3 *Time priority*   As the term suggests, this means that it is important to establish which factor in a causal relationship precedes the other in time. In some disciplines, such as history, this is not difficult. If one were exploring the influence of the French Revolution on twentieth century thought, then time priority is not problematical. But what of the so-called 'chicken and egg' situation one finds so often in sociology? For instance, some people claim that marriages are weakened because normally domesticated women want to study at university. But could the causal influence be the reverse where, as a result of a shaky marriage, women want to study? Whether there is only one cause of women entering university or whether this theory is true is beside the point. It is the having of the cause and the thing caused in the right order which is important, a requirement which, as we can see, is not always easy to satisfy.

4 *Discreteness of the independent and dependent variables*
This is a technical way of saying that before you can be sure two variables are causally related you need to be sure that you actually have two variables which are not facets of the same thing. An obvious example would be the claim that storms are caused by dreadful weather! It is easy to see that both variables are aspects of the same event. However, not all examples in social science are so obvious. Of the many criticisms of Weber's *The Protestant Ethic and the Spirit of Capitalism*, some include the claim that the variables — the protestant ethic and the spirit of capitalism — were really both facets of the same broad orientation to the world which was current at the time. Again, the truth of this claim is not immediately important. The lesson is knowing what to look for when one asks 'might these variables be a part of the same thing?'

5 *Non spuriousness*   As we saw earlier, this exists when the association between two factors, such as the level of smoking and the likelihood of contracting lung cancer, is not the result of a third and independent factor. This criterion of a causal argument is often the most difficult to establish simply because of the unknown role of independent factors. Using *The Protestant Ethic and the Spirit of Capitalism* as our example again, the causal relationship Weber posited between these two factors has been criticised as a spurious relationship because they were the effects of another third factor which was related to the nature of central, political control (see Swanson 1967).

Having briefly listed the key criteria of a causal argument, it is important to stress that satisfaction of all five criteria does not automatically guarantee the existence of causality. However, unless these criteria are met, there are no reasonable grounds for assuming such a relationship.

Concepts and degrees of abstraction

Mentioning instances where insufficient evidence prevents the establishment of a causal relationship provides a useful stepping stone to the final section of this chapter, which involves looking closely at the nature of concepts and **abstraction**. Put differently, on some occasions it is not possible to claim causality because there is insufficient evidence to demonstrate covariation or association of highly abstract concepts. One could imagine, for example, the possibility of a doctor gathering sufficient evidence to demonstrate that a patient is vomiting partly due to factors such as the presence of a particular bacteria or the result of a motor car accident. However, comparatively speaking, it is fairly clear that difficulty in gathering the right sort of evidence would prevent a straightforward testing of the proposition that most human illnesses are influenced to some extent by the human will to live. But why would there be this difficulty? It is because the proposition is couched in abstract concepts.

Let us first examine the notion of 'concepts'. Many methodology texts note that concepts are pictures or images of reality (e.g. see Rose 1982: 34ff.). Without getting involved in linguistic analysis, we can say that concepts are terms in our language with which we manipulate the external world. When a patient complains about a 'headache' or 'nausea', these concepts are manipulating or packaging what that person feels and enable meaningful communication of the symptoms they represent. I say 'meaningful' because these sorts of everyday concepts have meanings we all understand implicitly. In other words, we take their use and meaning for granted and rarely dwell upon their communicative nature. To further this point, consider what would happen to our everyday concepts if any of us were shipwrecked and forced to spend a lengthy period alone on an island. No doubt the body would still have its various aches and pains but such an isolated individual would gradually lose his/her repertoire of concepts to describe them. The more 'complex' the concepts, the quicker we would forget them. So, two related points emerge concerning concepts: they are both communicative and meaningful. These points are obviously related because concepts can only communicate meaning if their audience already understands the nature of those meanings.

The notion of 'meaning' and 'meaningful' is not always understood in this context and is therefore worth a comment. Take, for instance, the term 'love'. I deliberately say 'term' rather than 'concept' because the concept of love is really many concepts. Here we have an instance of the same word conveying several different meanings depending on its use or context:

'I fell in love',
'I love humankind',
'I love animals',
'I love Chinese food',
'I love driving fast cars'.

In each case the same word conveys a different image or picture of reality. In other words, each use of the term has a different meaning. It is because we all understand those meanings that we are able to use those terms correctly to communicate with each other. To stress the notion of 'concepts', there are also those situations in which we use different terms but are really using the same concept. We often use different expressions, such as, 'vet', 'vetinarian', 'animal doctor' or 'vetinary surgeon', but with the one concept in mind. Similarly, stop signs in different countries have different terms painted on them, but they are all conveying the same image or concept.

Using this broad understanding of concepts, let us proceed by turning to what we mean by 'degrees of abstraction'. We saw earlier that we are able to communicate because we share meanings of the concepts we have at our disposal. However, the extent to which we all truly share those meanings is a more–or–less phenomenon. We all understand the meaning of 'cup' or 'dog', for example, but what of concepts used in nuclear physics, such as 'meson'; or concepts used in other languages, such as, 'bella figura'; or even concepts in fiction which appear unfathomable, such as the concept of 'folding space' used by Frank Herbert in *Dune*? Often the meaning of these concepts is beyond us because of their degree of abstraction. That is to say, they can only be understood in terms of other concepts, which, in turn, require understanding in terms of more concepts and so on. An illustration should make this point clear. When we ask 'what is a cup?' we could be shown a cup and told 'this is a cup' or, more likely, we could be told that 'a cup is a receptacle for drinking purposes'. To grasp what 'cup' means from this statement we would have to know the meaning of 'receptacle' and 'drinking purposes'. If we did not, then the meaning of these concepts, or sub concepts, would have to be spelled out in terms of more sub concepts. Or, we could be given a simple demonstration of someone drinking from a cup to convey the point. Even with the most unfamiliar concepts, we eventually grasp their meaning by using levels of sub concepts. The extent to which there are levels of sub concepts between a concept and that to which it refers in the world can be regarded as levels of abstraction.

A simple way of understanding the idea of levels of abstraction is to ask how many sentences would it take to explain an unfamiliar concept to someone from another culture? If, for example, alongside of 'cup' we look at the concept of 'love', we see that it is possible to convey the meaning of 'cup' using a relatively smaller number of sentences than would be required to convey what 'love' meant. Figure 1.7 attempts to demonstrate this point.

Given we have different levels of abstraction, why is it that we appear to create unnecessary complexity by formulating concepts at the higher rather than the lower levels of abstraction? Would it not be simpler to cope in life with concepts like 'cup' rather than those with the level of abstraction of 'love'? The short answer to this question is 'no'. We use

| | **Level of abstraction** | |
	HIGH	*LOW*
	'LOVE'	'CUP'
Theoretical domain (concepts)	Passionate affection involving another person. Can also be directed to something. ⇓	A receptacle used for drinking purposes. ⇓
	'Passionate' means intense emotion. ⇓	A 'receptacle' is . . . ⇓
	'Affection' means having tender feelings towards someone. ⇓	'Drinking purposes' means . . .
	'Tender feelings' are . . . ⇓	⇓
	Requires many sentences to convey meaning because ⇓	*Requires few sentences to convey meaning because* ⇓
Empirical domain (evidence)	*cannot give an instance* — *cannot say* 'This is a 'passionate'', or 'This is an 'affection''.	*can give an instance* — 'This is a cup . . .', or 'This is its use' (demonstrate by drinking from a cup).

Figure 1.7 *Illustration of levels of abstraction*

levels of abstraction or, more–or–less abstract concepts, to enable us to manipulate more aspects of our reality. When a doctor says that illness is influenced by the will to live, we see that this sort of statement is on a fairly high level of abstraction. Without putting too fine a point on the precise level, it is deliberately pitched at this level to make a global statement about human illness rather than one about the health of a few individuals. Hence, abstract concepts, such as 'illness', 'the will to live' and even 'influenced', which we know to be a synonym for '(partly) caused', are shorthand terms manipulating a variety of many events in the world so that we can understand them as a unity.

The final aspects of abstraction which need discussing are 'nominal' and 'operational' definitions. They not only illuminate the notion of abstraction but are also important when it comes to understanding the link between theory and evidence, which is the substance of the next chapter. Nominal definitions are those which use sub concepts to define a concept so that its meaning is clear. We might accept that the nominal definition of 'cup' is 'a receptacle for drinking purposes' just as we might define 'love' as 'passionate affection of one person for another but also refers to deep affection or attachment to something' (such as our earlier examples of Chinese cooking and driving fast cars). Operational definitions, on the other hand, are those which provide an instance of the concept. An operational definition of 'cup' would be satisfied by pointing to an instance of it. So, in response to the question 'what is an X?', nominal definitions can be thought of as those sorts of statements which complete the sentence 'An X is . . . ', whereas operational definitions state 'This is an X' and point to an instance of it. Understanding of the notion of abstraction comes from our observation that some concepts are on such a high level of abstraction that it becomes difficult, or even impossible, to denote or derive an instance of them. The importance of the necessity of this link between the nominal and operational definition will become evident in the next chapter.

NOTES

1 Hempel illustrates the notion of 'ideal scientific inquiry' by quoting A. B. Wolfe, 'Functional economics' in Tugwell (ed), *The Trend of Economics*, New York, Alfred A. Knopf Inc., 1924. Wolfe's account of 'the scientific method' is a four stage process: (i) observation, (ii) analysis and classification, (iii) inductive derivation of generalisations, and (iv) further testing of generalisations. Commentaries on the scientific method often vary in their location of the starting point of research, but this is not of consequence for this book; cf. Figure 1.2.

2 Youngson is quoting R. J. Godlee, *Lord Lister*, Oxford, 1924, pp. 483–85.

2
The Nature of Social Science Research

In the previous chapter, social science was defined as the attempt to explain social phenomena within the limits of available evidence. This nexus between theory and evidence cannot be overly stressed and will become clearer in this chapter. I deliberately say 'nexus', rather than merely noting that this chapter will focus on theory *and* evidence, because it is not possible to understand theory nor evidence independently of each other. To have a theory is to have a theory about some thing: to have evidence is to have evidence for something of a theoretical or explanatory nature! This chapter will begin to use more examples of social science research to clarify this key principle of methodology but, first, it is important to present a broad picture of the trends of that research.

Common trends in social science research
All social science research differs in terms of four broad dimensions:
- **(i)** type of approach to theory
- **(ii)** type of approach to evidence
- **(iii)** type of method
- **(iv)** type of concepts employed.

Although they are not listed in any particular order, the inter-relationships of these dimensions form a distinct pattern or trend. Before addressing what this means, it is necessary to briefly to say something about each dimension.

Type of approach to theory We characterise social science

research as either 'theory testing' or 'theory construction'. Strictly speaking, we should say *mainly* theory testing or theory construction because research is rarely totally one or the other, as will become obvious later in this chapter.

Type of approach to evidence Researchers have differing assumptions about the conditions surrounding social evidence. Some believe that evidence is not evidence unless it can be quantified, that is, measured in precise units. By contrast, other researchers see the only important evidence for social scientists as residing in the thinking, rational human and, hence, consisting of more qualitative elements such as feelings, thoughts and meanings. The arguments surrounding each assumption are lengthy and will not be rehearsed in this section. However, again, these approaches are more–or–less phenomena, with researchers adopting mainly the 'quantitative approach' or the 'qualitative approach' to evidence.

Type of method This refers to the method(s) used to collect evidence. As we shall see shortly, a certain approach to evidence is often accompanied by a particular method of collecting it.

Type of concepts employed Social scientists use two types of concepts to explain social phenomena — their own and/or those of the subjects they study. The former are often referred to as 'observer's concepts' and the latter as 'participant's concepts'. A very good illustration of an observer's concept is Marx's notion of 'false consciousness'. This concept is by definition an observer's concept because not only is it Marx's creation, but is also, given its meaning, never used by the subjects it refers to. By contrast, participant's concepts are the very terms subjects use to make sense of their social reality, which the social scientist then incorporates in an explanation. Using this type of concept, a study of a religious community, for example, would attempt to explain, say, change to a new lifestyle by using each participant's own account. No doubt the meaningful concepts would include terms such as 'sin', 'salvation', 'rebirth' and 'revelation'.

Variation of types of concept is not unique t
ence. Like many of the principles of methodology
illustrations are found in everyday life, such as in n
the courtroom. If a doctor wants to arrive at an ex
or diagnosis for a particular illness, then the reaso
final diagnosis may concentrate on the doctor's cᴏ.ᴄpts,
that is, 'signs' such as haemoglobin level, blood pressure and
other test results. On the other hand, one can imagine other
paths to a final diagnosis which focus more on 'symptoms' or
what the patient feels, such as 'I always feel anxious', 'I
constantly feel hot then cold' and 'I have this gnawing pain in
the centre of my abdomen'. Successful diagnosis of some
diseases is only possible using the patient's or participant's
concepts.

These dimensions are inter-related in such a way that
patterns are clearly observable. In other words, a certain
approach to theory is often accompanied by a particular
approach to evidence and so on, patterns which are evident
in Figure 2.1. The two patterns indicated are certainly not
the only ones in social research, but they provide a good idea
of a range of important methodological principles. The
patterns are illustrated by the heavy arrows while the lighter
arrows indicate that it is logically possible to have any
combination of the contents of these dimensions.

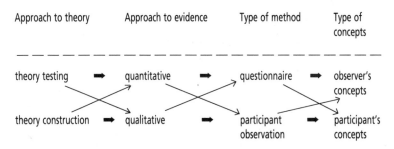

Figure 2.1 *The dimensions of social research — two
significant patterns*

ᴊttern 1 — Theory testing research

Much of what follows in this and the following section is inspired by Rose's (1982) A to E model of social research. The departure is that I have elaborated on what is implicit in Rose to assist the beginner.

It is first important to have a general picture of Rose's A to E model. As Figure 2.2 indicates, this model specifies the key areas of theory testing research and their order of execution. A more detailed understanding of these areas will emerge but at this stage it is important merely to note that Figure 2.2 is

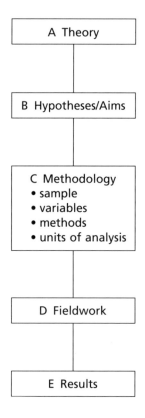

Figure 2.2 *Rose's model of theory testing research*

saying that theory testing research starts with a particular theory (A). In order to test this theory, hypotheses need to be generated (B). The content of these hypotheses points to the sorts of decisions which need to be made about what will count as evidence and how it will be gathered (C). The task of gathering evidence is carried out (D) and is then ordered and analysed (E) to see whether it supports the theory or not. I deliberately say that it is important 'merely to note' what this figure is saying: understanding it is the next task. This end will be served by using both Figures 2.2 and 2.3 when following the text.

THE THEORY

Starting with a theory is not a difficult notion to grasp. Earlier in the preamble, I suggested that we all understand what is happening when a doctor says 'I think the patient has hepatitis but I will need to do some tests to confirm it', or when the prosecutor in a courtroom asserts that the accused committed the crime and that evidence will be produced to demonstrate this claim. In each case the starting point is a theory and what follows is an attempt to see whether it is the case or not. The principle is the same in the theory testing pattern of social science research. It would not be unusual to find sociologists, for example, starting with Durkheim's theory of suicide (or a modification of it) as a possible explanation of a high or changing suicide rate in a particular location (e.g. see Coser 1976). Basically, the sociologist is saying 'I think Durkheim's theory of suicide could well be the explanation of what has been happening in this place. I will need to do some research to see whether it is the case'.

Let us suppose that the theory the sociologist is wanting to test is a modification of Durkheim and is being used to see whether it is the explanation for a sudden rise in the suicide rate in a particular suburb. With a little licence, let us state it in one sentence:

Suicide rates in defined localities are generally influenced
by individuals' degree of social integration.

There are a couple of comments to add before teasing out
the steps of testing this theory. First, this single sentence is
the 'short form' of the theory. It is extracted from the 'long
form', which could be anything up to a book length account
of the nature of the key concepts, their relationships, and the
evidence for the theory being formulated in the first place.
Doctors give patients a similar short form of explanation for
their symptoms when they offer a diagnosis. 'Pneumonia',
'diabetes' or 'coronary heart disease', for instance, make
sense to most patients as explanations of their respective
problems but, as a glance at the appropriate medical texts
would indicate, each diagnosis is accompanied by more complex details of changes in anatomy and physiology. In fact, it
is only through knowledge of these and other changes that
doctors know how to distinguish one disease from another
and how intervene with treatment.

A second comment is that the short form of this hypothetical theory of suicide is telling us that in social situations the
degree of social integration is generally an influence on suicide rates. It is, therefore, *not* saying that social integration is
a necessary condition of suicide. Put into the language we
used in the previous chapter, suicide rates are influenced by
several factors, each of which is, most likely, neither a necessary nor sufficient condition in the causal picture.

Returning to the process of theory testing, consider the
difference between our theory of suicide and another hypothetical theory — the presence of a rock band as an explanation for the noise in an adjoining room. If one were asked to
test the latter theory, it would be a straightforward matter
simply to have a look to see if it was in fact a rock band or just
a noisy radio or some other source of noise. Turning to our
theory of suicide, why is it not possible to test it in the same
manner? This comparison is highlighted by the earlier discussion of abstraction, especially the content of Figure 1.7. It

is not possible to directly test the theory of suicide for the same reason as it is not possible to point to a 'love'. As we saw, love is not a concrete thing but an abstract term which stands for (or abstracts) a number of qualities of social situations. It requires spelling out in terms of sub concepts so that we can recognise empirical instances to which the concept can be applied. By contrast, a 'cup', like a rock band, is a concrete thing. We simply need to look to see an instance of it or, in the language of the previous chapter, having a nominal definition quickly enables location of an operational definition of it. In short, because the abstract sociological concepts of 'suicide rate' and 'social integration' and the medical diagnosis 'pneumonia' are not concrete things and, therefore, are not directly observable, they can only be grasped indirectly. This involves producing testable propositions or hypotheses.

THE HYPOTHESES

Put simply, hypotheses are propositions which accord with simple propositional logic; that is, if this theory is true, then I should be able to observe the following things (if A then B). Take the case of pneumonia, for example. As a disease it cannot be observed directly, that is, a doctor cannot directly observe 'a pneumonia'. So, a doctor's logic is identical to the 'if A, then B' model above, that is, if this person has pneumonia, then I can expect to confirm the following testable propositions or hypotheses:

(a) there will be pneumococci bacteria in the sputum;
(b) the patient will exhibit certain chest sounds when examined with a stethoscope;
(c) the patient will have a certain pattern of body temperature change; and
(d) the patient will describe a particular mode of onset of symptoms.

Based on this medical analogy, how might our theory of suicide be tested? We cannot directly observe suicide rates nor the process of social integration, so what would one expect to observe if those concepts were related, as the theory holds? Since we are dealing with a hypothetical theory, we do not have its actual long form to direct us. However, in principle, we can say that the source of hypotheses is the nature of the evidence on which the theory was originally based. In proposing his theory of suicide, Durkheim observed the empirical world, abstracted or refined certain elements related to suicide and then proposed an explanation using concepts he created. Developing hypotheses involves the reverse of this process, that is, moving from the theory back towards the sort of evidence supporting it. We know from a careful reading of Durkheim's *Suicide* that the original evidence for the concept of social integration has to do with the nature of individuals' social connectedness. Religion binds people together to certain standards and, according to Durkheim, Catholics are more socially integrated than Protestants because religion occupies and governs more of their lives. Based on this assumption, and given that Durkheim's work is guiding our hypothetical theory, we could propose the following hypotheses concerning the suburb with the recently elevated suicide rate:

(a)   in this suburb the proportion of people with religious commitment has declined recently;

(b)   suicide victims are mainly non practising believers or people with no religion.

Of course, these are not the only hypotheses one could test. Durkheim acknowledged other aspects of social connectedness, such as membership of organisations. Assuming that a high rate of organisational membership implies a high degree of social integration and vice versa, then again the following testable propositions could be derived:

(a)   in this suburb organisational membership has recently declined;

and, incorporating the religious dimension;

(b)   in this suburb organisational membership among committed religious believers has recently declined.

Of course, these hypotheses do not address why there should be a decline in the proportion of believers and/or a similar decline in organisational membership. That would involve another causal theory. For the moment, the hypotheses are simply attempting to test whether a decline in social integration accounts for the elevated suicide rate.

So, following the logic of 'if this theory is true, then this is what I expect to find', a word of caution is warranted. If the hypotheses are eventually found to be true, it does not logically follow that the theory is true. There could be some other explanation for the hypotheses being confirmed. The patient with suspected pneumonia, whose tests were all indicative of that disease, could have had a some other chest malady, just as changing suicide rates have different causes in different places. The best one can say when all hypotheses are confirmed is that the theory is more *credible* but not necessarily true. On the other hand, if all the hypotheses are found to be false, then we can say with more confidence that the theory is false.

Such confidence follows the basic claims of propositional logic (e.g. see Salmon 1963). Without opening up a complex philosophical discussion, it may be of assistance to have the main guideposts of that logic. Beginning with hypotheses found to be false, the reasoning is as follows:

If the theory to be tested is true, then one could expect to confirm hypothesis B.	If A then B.
Hypothesis B is found to be false, therefore the theory is false.	Not B, therefore not A.

This process of reasoning is known as 'denying the consequent' and, because it is a valid argument, is the only sure test of the theory. 'Valid' here means that something follows from something else. So, assuming the theory were true and that the hypothesis logically derives from the theory but is, in fact, untrue, then it follows that the theory is untrue. By contrast, we cannot be as confident of the truth of the theory if we confirm the same hypothesis. This is evident in the reasoning which one might be tempted to use:

If the theory to be tested is true, then one could expect to confirm hypothesis B.	If A then B.
Hypothesis B is found to be true, therefore the theory is true.	B, therefore A.

This, at first glance, might look a reasonable argument but 'affirming the antecedent', as it is known, is invalid. The following example demonstrates why:

If it rains, then the function will be cancelled.	If A then B.
The function was cancelled, therefore it rained.	B, therefore A.

Hence, compared to the confidence we have when a hypothesis is found to be false, confirmation only allows us to assume that the theory is, to use Stinchcombe's (1968: 15–28) words, 'more credible'.

This talk of hypotheses being true or false is a little premature although warranted at this point. Understanding what happens if all hypotheses are true or false assists in grasping the logic of the test of the theory. But how do we actually test a hypothesis? We have already noted that a hypothesis is a testable proposition whereas the theory is not, but is there not still a problem when it comes to testing the proposition that 'suicide victims are mainly non practising believers or people with no religion'?

It would appear that there is still the same problem of not being able to directly observe concepts such as 'non practising believers' and 'people with no religion'. This is admittedly the case, but the point is that the image of reality conveyed by these sub concepts is readily understood by social scientists in terms of what is actually happening in the world. So, although they are not concrete entities, researchers have a good idea of what to do to test the truth of the hypotheses in which they are located. Having 'a good idea of what to do' implies decision making in terms of what will count as evidence. It is this decision making which leads us into the next stage — stage C. Rose (1982) calls it 'operationalisation'.

OPERATIONALISATION — MAKING DECISIONS ABOUT EVIDENCE

As its awkward name implies, 'operationalisation' involves making decisions as to what will count as evidence for the sub concepts in the hypotheses. This is the point at which theory and evidence first meet and is the most vulnerable aspect of theory testing research because of the nature of the decisions to be made. The problematical nature of the theory–evidence link is evident in many methodology texts where it is often referred to as the 'concept–indicator problem' (see Rose 1982). 'Indicator' refers to the sort of evidence which indicates the existence of the concept. In other words, it is a case of having a concept and then deciding on an indicator 'to get at it'. As Rose's model indicates, these decisions are made in terms of

- method to be used
- sample
- variables
- units of analysis

These areas are closely linked so that decisions about each are not necessarily made in any order. Our medical analogy will illustrate this decision making, and the continuing story of the test of the theory of suicide will also show the modifications required in social research.

Taking the medical hypotheses first, what sorts of decisions are required in terms of the above areas? For the sake of convenience, let us take just one hypothesis which attempts to establish the truth of the theory or diagnosis of pneumonia, that is, 'there will be pneumococci bacteria in the sputum'. Based on the above discussion in the section on hypotheses, it is clear that although pneumococci are not directly observable an expert would know exactly what to do to test this proposition. Without labouring the details, the method chosen might be a microscopic examination of a sample of sputum. The **sample** of sputum is not problematical because any sample of the patient's sputum is likely to contain as many bacteria as any other. The variables would be the presence or absence of characteristic shapes under the microscope and possibly their number or concentration, while the **units of analysis** or individual units of evidence actually scrutinised would be visual microscopic images. One does not have to be a doctor to see that all this is routine. However, this routine everyday practice illustrates an important aspect of the methodology of social research. Before turning to the test of the theory of suicide, it is worth looking again, but in diagramatic form, at what has happened in the test of this medical hypothesis. The picture in Figure 2.3 shows how decisions concerning the hypotheses to be tested, the method, sample and so on progressively translate a theoretical or conceptual statement into an empirical one.

The process of decision making to test a medical hypothesis might seem somewhat straightforward — it is. This is largely because of its routine nature and, above all, the fact that it works in terms of allowing doctors to prescribe the appropriate treatment. Nevertheless, the assumptions surrounding this process and the types of decisions and associated difficulties are identical to those in social research, a point covered by the test of our hypothesis derived from the theory of suicide (see Fig. 2.3).

Taking just one hypothesis, what decisions are required to operationalise the proposition that 'suicide victims are mainly non practising believers or people with no religion'? We noted earlier that this sort of statement is more concrete than the theory itself and, therefore, social scientists have 'a good idea' of how to proceed to test it. The following rationale summarises the sort of decision making one would expect to see in this situation:

	SOCIOLOGY	MEDICINE
Long form of theory	Lengthy account of study with details of concepts.	Detailed medical account of disease processes.
A. Short form of theory to be tested	Suicide rates are generally influenced by individuals' degree of social integration.	Pneumonia.
B. Hypothesis generation	Suicide victims are mainly non practising believers or people with no religion.	There will be pneumococci bacteria in the sputum.
C. Operational-isation	Respondents' answers to questions will indicate that most individuals seen to have committed suicide will not have in their personal effects evidence of religious affiliation nor will clergy have been present at the time of identification of the victim.	There will be images of a particular shape and concentration in a microscopic examination of a drop of patient's sputum.
D. Carrying out the collection of evidence/ fieldwork	Response rate not as high as anticipated — only 75%.	Microscopic examination carried out — no problems encountered in preparing slides etc.
E. Results	Just over half of suicide victims had no evidence of religious memorabilia in their personal effects. Three quarters of suicide victims' relatives were unaccompanied by clergy at the time of identification. *Conclusion:* hypothesis confirmed, therefore, theory that suicide rates are generally influenced by the degree of social integration is more credible.	There were 10,000 images of a characteristic shape per unit area of the microscope slide. *Conclusion:* images' shape and concentration consistent with presence of pneumococci bacteria. Hypothesis confirmed, therefore stronger grounds for believing patient has pneumonia.

Figure 2.3   *Broad picture of theory testing in sociology and medicine*

The difficulties of studying suicide face all social scientists. At an obvious level, the researcher cannot interview nor observe suicide victims, so all evidence must, to some extent, be of an indirect nature. A more subtle level of difficulty concerns the concept of 'suicide': how do we know we are getting at what we think we are getting at? How do we know that our indicators of suicide are actually measuring the existence and full extent of this phenomenon? The reluctance of kin to admit the existence of a suicide in the family and the apparent, similar reluctance of coroners to return a finding of suicide in situations where suicide is known to be the cause of death make the recording of the true rate of suicide in any location a difficult task. Relatives are loathe to admit its existence and coroner's court records underestimate its incidence. For these reasons we will attempt to ascertain the true rate of suicide by interviewing morgue attendants in the suburb under scrutiny. Using a prepared **questionnaire**, this method should yield accurate evidence of the incidence of suicide in that place because the sample, who have already agreed to cooperate, just happens to constitute 95% of the thirty or so attendants employed in the suburb's morgues. They have all indicated a willingness to cooperate, partly encouraged by the local authorities' permission for the attendants to be interviewed. Given political sensitivity of the sudden increase of suicide in this suburb, authorities agreed to allow attendants to take part in the study knowing that they were going to with or without permission. The special advantage of interviewing attendants, apart from their willingness to cooperate, is that no two or more of them will be reporting on the same case of suicide. Given their work practices and shifts, each has a different 'list' to report, which maximises accuracy in determining the exact number of suicides in a given period. The variables will be attendants' responses to the questions on the questionnaire, which aim to establish not only the existence of a suicide but also the nature and extent of religious affiliation. The latter property is indicated by questions which tap each attendant's knowledge of religious artifacts in the victim's personal effects and the presence or absence of clergy at the time relatives identified the victim. Responses to these questions would constitute the units of analysis.

Disregarding the somewhat macabre nature of this example, it illustrates the decisions taken to translate the concepts of 'suicide', 'non practising believer' and '(individuals with) no religion' into empirical indicators which can be directly observed.

CARRYING OUT THE RESEARCH AND ANALYSING THE RESULTS

Imagine further that the research is carried out and that a less than expected response rate is obtained from the attendants, that is, 75% rather than the promised 95%. Analysis of attendants' responses show that just over half of the suicide victims had no evidence of religious memorabilia in their personal effects and three quarters of relatives were unaccompanied by clergy at the time of identification of the victim. Confining ourselves for the moment to the wording of the hypothesis and its operationalisation, we can say that the hypothesis is confirmed, which makes the theory that suicide rates are influenced by the degree of social integration more credible (see Fig. 2.3).

A CRITICAL LOOK AT THIS EXAMPLE OF THEORY TESTING

But is this test of the hypothesis as straightforward as it looks? The theory surrounding suicide was deliberately chosen not only because it is a real topic which sociologists frequently investigate, but also because it presents us with probably more problems than any other research topic. The main problem lies in the operationalisation stage. In making decisions at this level, we had to establish indicators of suicide and the nature of religious affiliation. Decisions concerning the former were designed to be relatively sound, whereas those surrounding the latter were deliberately flawed.

Without entering into a lengthy debate about the merits of the indicators of suicide in this hypothetical study, it is sufficient to say that morgue attendants' familiarity with the day to day, informal aspects of their work is possibly the best source of evidence for the real causes of death of the people they handle. Therefore, assuming attendants' truthfulness, a matter to which we will return when we discuss question- naires in more detail, questions which 'get at' this evidence are good indicators of the extent of suicide. If the questions were:

1   How many cases of death were you required to deal with last month?
2   Which of those cases were, in your view, suicides? Why?

then there are good grounds for believing that these ques- tions would be getting at the extent of suicide and little else. Of course in reality the main difficulties in doing this sort of study would likely involve:

(a)   a smaller number of attendants being responsible for a given locality;
(b)   those attendants would not necessarily deal with all deaths, and therefore all suicides, in that locality; and
(c)   they would probably not be so willing to cooperate.

To say that decisions concerning indicators of the extent of suicide are 'relatively sound' indicates that those attempting to measure 'non practising believer' and 'people with no religion' are not. In what way then is the operationalisation of the latter pair of concepts flawed?

   The best way to begin assessing the soundness of indica- tors of abstract concepts like 'non practising believer' and 'person with no religion' is to remember that these indicators are the only link between the concept and its evidence. Accordingly, we should ask 'what could go wrong in using these indicators so that we end up not getting at what we think we are getting at?' As we have already noted, the indicators of the extent of suicide do not leave much room for getting at anything other than what they were designed to measure. Disregarding truthfulness for the moment, there are few (mis)interpretations of the possible answers to those questions. By contrast, let us examine the indicators of the concepts of religious affiliation. Imagine the precise questions were:

1   Was there any evidence of religious memorabilia, such as a pendant, a cross or a bible, among the personal effects of each of the cases of death you have been associated with in the past month? If so, what was the nature of that evidence?

2   At the time relatives identified each case, on which occasions were clergy present?

Keeping in mind that these questions are the only link with the concepts they are designed to indicate, what (mis) interpretations could one make of the answers? Consider the following:

(i)   The first question assumes the respondent is able to recognise all instances of religious memorabilia. Those non believing respondents may not be aware of more subtle artifacts, such as symbols on jewellery;

(ii)   The first question assumes that the presence of religious memorabilia indicates religious belief. This might be the case, but it says nothing about the extent to which the person concerned was a practising believer;

(iii) The absence of such memorabilia does not necessarily mean that the person was a non believer nor a non practising believer;

(iv) The second question assumes that the deceased was a believer if relatives were accompanied by clergy at the identification. Several interpretations of this situation exist. It could be that relatives are the believers rather than the victim. By contrast, the victim could have been either a practising or a non practising believer. How does one know?

(v)   The second question assumes that clergy do not attend if the deceased was not a believer. This is not necessarily the case. Clergy could attend, for example, as a favour to friends, who may be believers or non believers.

It is clear from this less than exhaustive list of possible

misinterpretations of answers to both questions that these indicators would not allow a researcher to 'get at' the concepts of 'non practising believer' and/or 'no religion'. This 'getting at what you think you are getting at' warrants a comment at this point. In methodology texts, the issue of whether an indicator follows from the concept it is designed to measure is usually discussed under the heading of 'validity'. Using an analogy, it is a little like a doctor trying to use a thermometer to measure a patient's blood pressure. It is perfectly obvious that 'it does not follow' that a reading on the thermometer indicates something about blood pressure. It would not be a valid indicator of what one is trying to 'get at'.

However, validity should not be confused with **reliability**, which is the extent to which any method of research will consistently deliver the same results when administered under the same conditions. In the case of our doctor and the thermometer, it may be the case that on every occasion the thermometer in question gives the same reading under the same circumstances. Even if our doctor believes those readings indicate blood pressure, we can say that the the thermometer is reliable. On the other hand, doctors who use a thermometer to measure or 'get at' body temperature are treating its reading as a valid indicator even if they are unaware that the thermometer is not reliable. The key point to emerge from this discussion is that in social research, as in all research, it is crucial to ensure that all methods used to obtain evidence are both reliable and valid indicators of what they are designed to measure.

Moving to the execution of the research, we have already noted that 75% rather than the promised 95% of morgue attendants were finally interviewed. What are the implications of this lower response rate? Without putting too fine a point on the precise rate, there is an obvious point the critical analyst, including the researcher, should be aware of. It basically amounts to the answer to the question 'who were the 25% who did not respond?' Although we can only speculate with this hypothetical piece of research, the message is twofold: (i) establish, if possible, who are the missing respondents, and then (ii) ascertain in what way their absence could make a difference to the results. In our suicide study it could be the case that the 25% of attendants who did not respond are very truthful people and, in light of the sensitivity of the problem of suicide, they did not want to be saying things which might incriminate their employers and others. By contrast, the 75% who did respond might be people who do not mind glossing the truth. If such a situation were the case, then it is clear that the results would be distorted and would present a skewed picture of what was actually happening regarding suicide. This is another case of not getting at what you think you are getting at; only this time, irrespective of the validity of the indicators in the questionnaire, the results would not be measuring what the indicators were meant to indicate.

Another problem surrounds the nature of the results, which reveal in part that three quarters of relatives were unaccompanied by clergy at the time of identification of the victim. Here we see an instance of the results not corresponding with the operationalised proposition. As a reminder, note that the latter is concerned with the *proportion of identifications* at which clergy are present whereas the conclusion is concerned with the *proportion of relatives* accompanied by clergy. It could be the case that the results have been arrived at by dividing the total number of relatives by the number of clergy present on all occasions. Again, the stated results are not getting at what they were intended to measure.

This brief, critical examination of the stages of a hypothetical instance of theory testing research provides an outline of a strategy for analysis of research of this type. In the next chapter, the nature of analysis will be scrutinised more closely. Given the research orientation of this chapter, it is necessary now to look more carefully at the most common research method used in theory testing research — the questionnaire.

A CLOSER LOOK AT THE QUESTIONNAIRE

Methodological issues surrounding questionnaires are rarely spelled out clearly and simply. Given that questions are crucial because they are often the sole indicators of the concepts in the theory being tested, an awareness of the ways in which validity can be systematically weakened is important for the methodologist as well as the practitioner.

This discussion is not primarily concerned with the different types of questionnaires used in social research, the main ones being:

- interviewer administered
- self administered
- telephone questionnaire

There are many variations of these categories. All types of questionnaire can contain questions with a pre-determined range of answers, or open ended questions which allow respondents to use their own words. Self administered questionnaires are sometimes completed in the presence of a supervisory person but on other occasions are mailed to the respondent. Also, questionnaires can vary immensely in length, from very short schedules of, say, 20–30 minutes, to in-depth interviews lasting many hours. Consideration of the effects of each of these variations on validity is an important exercise. However, it is not the focus of this discussion because it is related more to the specialised aspects of method. Instead, I want to focus more on the fundamental issue of the strengths and weaknesses of questionnaires in principle, that is, regardless of how they are administered. This issue is brought to light by examining two important areas: the sensitivity and type of information sought in a questionnaire, and wording effects.

The sensitivity and type of information sought in a questionnaire can each affect the validity of questions as indicators of concepts. Looking first at sensitivity, it is a fairly straightforward claim to say that sensitive topics are areas in which respondents are likely to avoid giving a truthful answer to a researcher's question. To such questions they may give false answers, misleading answers or no answers at all. A somewhat extreme example illustrates this point. Imagine a researcher wanting to 'get at' the extent to which 'crime pays'; that is, the extent to which law breakers avoid detection and punishment for each of their crimes. Disregarding the difficulty of making contact with those people, it is obvious what the response would be to questions which asked for details of their undetected, illegal activities. Questions such as 'have you committed any murders this year?' would invite a polite 'no' at the best of times, a sharp contrast to a question at the other end of the sensitivity range, such as 'have you bought any paint in the last week?'

The effect of sensitivity of a topic on the propensity to lie or avoid the issue is not confined to social research. In the case of the law, perhaps the most obvious example is the question often asked of the accused during a trial — 'Did you commit the crime?' Given the consequences of a guilty verdict and, hence, the sensitivity of the issue covered by the question, most people witnessing such a trial would expect the accused always to answer 'no' irrespective of the strength of the prosecution's case. In the doctor's consulting room, similar avoidance or lying is not unexpected in response to questions which probe the nature of a patient's sexual practice where a sexually transmitted disease is suspected.

Although lawbreaking is an obvious sensitive area, some of the other areas in which social researchers experience patterns of avoidance are worth noting. Politics, religion and income are topics which require careful attention to the wording of questions to minimise sensitivity. For example, instead of confronting a respondent with the question 'how much do you earn?', we might 'tone it down' by asking something like 'which of the following income ranges best approximates your income?' Sexual matters are another sensitive area in which people are likely to be uncooperative or lie when questioned. It is this sensitivity that led Humphreys (1971) to study homosexual activity in men's toilets by locating 'clients' through their car registration numbers and later approaching them to participate in a social health survey. Embedded in the health survey questionnaire, which was part of an actual study, were key questions which aimed to provide important information on homosexual activity but which, arguably, clients thought were concerned with social health. Other sensitive areas include questions about age and, perhaps surprisingly, people's friendships. In short, the greater the sensitivity of the area, the greater the risk of respondents not answering truthfully and, hence, the lower the validity of those questions as indicators of concepts they are designed to measure.

Type of information sought in questionnaires varies immensely and this variation impinges on validity. Generally, questionnaires aim to gather one or more of the following types of information from respondents:

- current behaviour
- past behaviour
- attitudes to issues involving high commitment
- attitudes to issues involving low commitment
- future behaviour
- future attitudes

There are, of course, variations and extensions of this list but basically this short schema is comprehensive enough for our purposes. The significance of this variation of the type of information sought is evident in a few examples. Disregarding the issue of sensitivity of the area under study, consider the following list of questions which correspond to each of the six types of information:

- 'Are you currently a member of a sporting club?'
- 'Have you bought any paint in the past week?'
- 'Are you in favour of logging our forests for wood chips?'
- 'Do you believe that gas turbines should be serviced tri-annually?
- 'Will you ever have children?'
- 'Will you ever believe in euthanasia?'

It is clear that, in terms of getting at what you think you are getting at, a question about past behaviour is potentially a good indicator because it is attempting to tap something definite which has already happened. By contrast, a question about future attitudes is potentially less valid as an indicator for two reasons. First, attitudes are less definite events in people's lives alongside of their behaviour. Often we can remember what we did ten or twenty years ago but are less successful in recalling what attitudes we held at that time. Second, future events, whether it be attitudes or behaviour, are precarious to tap because all sorts of factors can impinge on people's lives to alter what they sincerely believe to be inevitable.

If we combine these comments about sensitivity of information and type of information sought, it is possible to produce an approximate guide to the degree of validity obtained when questions are used as indicators of concepts.

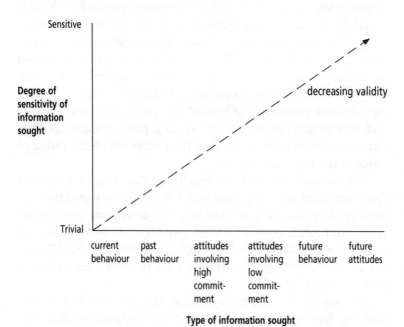

Figure 2.4 *A guide to validity of questions as indicators incorporating sensitivity and type of information sought*

Although no precise units of measurement exist, Figure 2.4 shows that when questions are worded to tap future attitudes on highly sensitive topics, there is low validity of those questions as indicators.

Wording effects also impinge on the validity of questions as indicators. Basically, a question cannot get at what a researcher intends if that question's wording is misinterpreted by the respondent.

A misinterpreted question, in effect, becomes a different question altogether. Of course, researchers generally do not deliberately set out to construct questions which can be misinterpreted and, therefore, the problem in administering questionnaires is that researchers are often unaware that respondents may be interpreting the same questions differently. The care needed in wording questions is presented by considering examples of each of the main wording problems:

(i) Ambiguity   This stems from two main wording problems. The first is the use of imprecise terms, such as 'average'. If a question asks 'What is the average price of houses in Sydney?' the term 'average' can be interpreted different ways. Although most people would probably interpret 'average' as the **mean** price of houses, people close to the housing industry would know that the 'average price' means **median** price, that is, the price which is the mid point in the range of prices under consideration.

The second type of ambiguity is the double barrelled question, that is, a question which is really two questions in one. A question, such as 'Do you like discussing your problems often with your parents?' (which I extracted from an actual questionnaire), is really two questions, that is, 'Do you *like discussing* your problems with your parents?' and 'Do you like to do this *often?*'

The key words in each question are in italics to indicate that the first is getting at whether the respondent likes discussing problems with parents, whereas the second is attempting to assess whether the respondent likes to do it often. The problem of ambiguity, however, is that many respondents perceive only one interpretation of this type of question, the end result being a range of responses which cover each interpretation. In some cases, the existence of a double barrelled question is discovered only after the questionnaire has been administered. Researchers often find that respondents actually write in their own comments on the questionnaire pointing out the double barrelled nature of the question. They might say something like: 'If the question means do I like discussing my problems with my parents, then my answer is definitely "yes". However, if the question is asking whether I like to do this often, then I think my answer is "no"'.

(ii) The amount of information given On some topics respondents are not well informed and the amount of background information in the question can influence the response. Take for example a question used in a McNair poll in Australia in the early 1970s. The question asked respondents

'Is the Government letting too many Asian people settle in Australia, or too few, or about the right number?'

No information was given as to the number of Asian people actually settled in Australia. Compare this question with another used in a Morgan poll in 1971.

'In 1971 3500 Asians were allowed to remain in Australia. How many Asians should be given permanent residential status each year?'

The information given in the second question can have the effect of correcting respondents' ignorance of the true situation. It would not be unusual to hear some respondents say, when asked the second question, 'Oh, is that all the Asians we let settle here. I thought the figure was more like 35000. If that is the case then I guess we really cannot complain about 3500 coming in'.

If it is appropriate and possible to provide this sort of information, then it can lead to respondents forming views on sound evidence rather than on ignorance or prejudice.

(iii) Legitimacy of the question   This is concerned with what respondents think interviewers want to hear rather than what they actually want to say. In many questionnaires the wording of the questions can give the respondent the impres-

Wording Effects of Referendum	Majority 'Yes' over 'No' among intending voters (%)
Do you accept the government's recommendation that the United Kingdom should come out of the Common Market?	+ 0.2
Should the United Kingdom come out of the Common Market? IN OUT	 + 4.6 +10.8
Should the United Kingdom stay in the Common Market?	+ 13.2
Do you accept the government's recommendations that the United Kingdom should stay in the Common Market?	+ 18.2
The government recommends the acceptance of the renegotiated terms of British membership of the Common Market. Should the United Kingdom stay in the Common Market?	+ 11.2
Her Majesty's government believes that the nation's best interests would be served by accepting the favourably negotiated terms of our continued membership of the Common Market. Should the United Kingdom stay in the Common Market?	+ 16.2

Figure 2.5   *Butler and Kitzinger's analysis of wording effects of questions on Britain's entry into the Common Market*

sion that a certain answer is desirable. The extent to which this type of wording effect can sway respondents is illustrated by Butler and Kitzinger's (1976: 60) analysis of the markedly divergent responses to differently worded questions about Britain's entry into the common market. Their Table 2, which is reproduced above as Figure 2.5, shows that, with increasing legitimacy of wording of the same basic question, the proportion of favourable responses increases.

(iv) Loaded questions   These involve the presence of key words which can sway responses in a certain direction. Sometimes these key words are added intentionally with the aim of producing a biased trend of responses. The question 'Are you willing to have reasonable price increases in the hope that they will lead to prosperity?' uses the word 'reasonable' in such a way as to make it difficult for anyone to answer 'no' because no one could object to anything which is reasonable!

(v) Leading questions   These assume that respondents have a definite opinion and thereby make it difficult for them to answer as they might think. The question 'Which is the better way to clear the forests — bulldozer or fire?' gives respondents, especially the environmentally conscious, no choices. Sometimes leading questions are more subtle, especially when they are exploring issues most people are sympathetic to. Note, for example, the assumption of an opinion in the following question:

'How do you feel that sex discrimination should be combatted?'

Whatever we might think about the issue of sex discrimination, good researchers should not assume that everyone believes it should be combatted.

The discussion to this point has provided a sufficiently detailed picture of the nature of theory testing research. An instructive contrast exists when it is placed alongside of the second pattern or trend in social science research — theory construction research.

Pattern 2 — Theory construction research

As the name suggests, theory construction research involves ending with a theory rather than starting with it. In other words, the doctor who says

> 'I think you have hepatitis and therefore we had better do some tests to confirm it.'

is starting with a theory, whereas another doctor who says,

> 'I don't know why you are ill so we will do some tests to find out just what is the matter.'

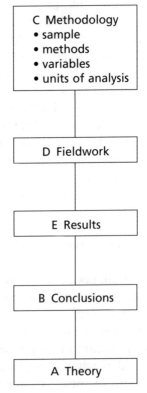

Figure 2.6 *Model of theory construction research based on modification of Rose's A to E model*

will, hopefully, end up with a theory or diagnosis. In this medical analogy, the fact that both approaches may use similar tests does not alter the fact that each has a different logic and mode of proceeding.

A useful starting point in this discussion is to identify the 'motor' or origin of theory construction research. If there is no theory to test, no hypotheses to guide the choice of method, sample and so on, what initiates this type of research? This question is raised when we recast Rose's A to E model of theory testing research to provide a visual representation of theory construction research. Figure 2.6 indicates research beginning with stage C and proceeding through stages D, E, B to A — the theory. If stage C is the starting point, then what guides the choice of the sample, method, variables and units of analysis? We saw in the previous chapter that evidence does not exist in isolation but is always evidence for something of a theoretical nature. What is that something in this situation? Again our medical and legal analogies will help to clarify the answer.

Suppose again you are back in your doctor's surgery and, in light of your recent illness, you are given the now familiar words,

'I don't know why you are ill so we will do some tests to find out just what is the matter.'

In this situation, even though a theory or diagnosis is not being tested, your doctor's mode of proceeding does not occur in a vacuum. Most people would be aware that the choice of pathology samples, the methods of analysing them, the variables and units of analysis are all guided by medical precedent or, in other words, the literature concerning this sort of blanket testing. Let us suppose that a variety of tests indicate you have a rare form of anaemia called Smith's Anaemia. This explanation of your recent ill health is well documented in the medical literature in that any informed person could easily see what is causing what in this particular disease. Based on this literature, your doctor proposes a form of treatment to which you quickly respond.

Generally, this is a familiar sort of situation where broad steps are easily understood. Fortunately, its simplicity allows us to grasp a fundamental principle of theory construction. That principle is that most cases of theory construction involve existing theories to which researchers must remain faithful. What do we mean by 'faithful'? In the medical analogy above, the doctor proposing Smith's Anaemia as the theory or explanation of your illness was being faithful to it in two ways:

(i) knowing that the tests pointed to Smith's Anaemia, he/she did not want to invent some other theory to account for a relatively rare state of affairs; and

(ii) if the tests had not clearly pointed to Smith's Anaemia, then it would not have been proposed as a diagnosis.

Theory construction in social science research follows the same principle. In our earlier hypothetical study of increased suicide in a particular suburb, if all the evidence exactly fitted Durkheim's description of 'low social integration', then it is important to remain faithful to Durkheim's theory by using that concept to characterise that situation rather than generating a new concept. On the other hand, if the evidence only vaguely approximated the indicators of 'social integration', then it would be unfaithful to apply this concept.

The only exception to this principle is when a researcher creates a theory for the first time because there is no other explanation to account for the evidence. In the case of your doctor doing a range of medical tests to see why you have been ill, it has been known for some individuals to have a disease not previously observed and, consequently, requiring naming. In this sort of situation the issue of faithfulness does not apply simply because there is nothing to be faithful to. In principle, there would be nothing to stop the doctor observing this new disease calling it the 'XYZ Disease' or the 'Mickey Mouse Malady'!

Creating concepts and theories from scratch, that is, *de*

novo, is more common in social science than it is in medicine, although it is probably not the dominant pattern. However, many of the concepts social scientists create are far from faithful in the sense in which I use this term above. This claim is somewhat peripheral to this introduction to methodology and, as it would involve a very lengthy discussion to defend it, I think I would prefer to see some social science graduate student take it up as a thesis topic.

A HYPOTHETICAL EXAMPLE OF THEORY CONSTRUCTION

To illustrate the steps in theory construction research, I want to develop a hypothetical example foreshadowed earlier. Imagine a social scientist, a sociologist, is interested in understanding why some apparently successful people give up their material wealth and enter an enclosed religious community. Why do they change from a comfortable, secure life-style to one which is outwardly austere and insecure? This question does not occur in a vacuum but is informed by a variety of insights in the literature on the sociology of religion — principally, the stress on 'pull' factors and 'push' factors.

Pull factors focus on what it is that individuals are attracted to and stem from addressing the question 'why is it that some individuals are attracted to a religious setting and not some other type of situation?' The main insight from this focus is the importance of understanding the individual's 'definition of the situation' at the time of entering the religious community. This sort of approach emphasises that individuals do not necessarily see the religious community they are entering as outsiders do, and it focuses on the participant's own concepts or accounts of the situation. Push factors, by contrast, are concerned with the nature of the social situation an individual leaves behind. The assumption here is that that situation contains factors which may be 'pushing' the individual out. Armed with these insights, it makes sense for our sociologist to wonder why some people make a sudden and dramatic change of lifestyle by entering religious communities. Is it because of push factors, pull factors or both?

As we have already noted, sociologists whose research falls into this pattern have certain assumptions about what will count as evidence. Unlike the quantitative approach to evidence, where evidence must be quantitatively measurable, the qualitative approach assumes that, because sociology is concerned with understanding human social behaviour, the best evidence is individuals' account of their own social behaviour. The best method is to tap what those individuals think by participating in their social world. Accordingly, our sociologist approaches a local monastery and obtains permission to attend daily and participate in its routine activities with the aim of answering the research questions above. Specifically, the *sample* is all the residents of a particular monastery. It is not necessarily representative of all monasteries but, rather, was chosen because of its location and the previous contact the sociologist had had with its superior. This sort of sample is often called a 'convenience sample'. The *method* is participant observation, about which we will say more later, and the *units of analysis* are the residents' accounts of their past and present lives complemented by the sociologist's observational notes of the nature of monastic life. The *variables* are difficult to specify before the evidence is collected but, in principle, they are the variable nature of those accounts concerning a variety of topics the sociologist wishes to explore. The precise nature of that variation can only be specified after the evidence is analysed. Let us imagine that the sociologist virtually lives in the monastery for six months observing and talking to residents about their change of lifestyle. We are later presented with a written account of the findings.

The sociologist declares that all residents were cooperative in the course of the research and that the findings are based on numerous interviews with each of twenty men. A theory is proposed that these men gave up their former lives because of push and pull factors. They were all pushed because their lives, albeit materially successful, were dominated by 'problems', such as 'irregular hours', 'missed meals', 'constantly travelling and living out of a suitcase', and 'not knowing what was likely to happen next in the work situation'. They were attracted or pulled to the monastic life because they were 'practising Christians – but not fanatics' who had 'a certain sympathy for that sort of life'.

Together, the push and pull factors support a theory which the sociologist calls 'the selective ritual theory'. This theory, put simply, is saying that certain men, no matter how successful they are, experience a problem with the lack of routine in their work lives. More to the point, the evidence suggests that they crave not just routines in the workplace but rituals, that is, routines with symbolic significance. They were initially attracted to the monastic life because it provides the ritual, as one monk put it, 'we, as a group, generally need'. Life in the monastery 'is ordered', 'is planned so that you know what you should be doing at any one time' and 'is not boring even though you do the same thing every day' were typical comments. The 'selective' aspect of this theory stems from the fact that all were professed practising Christians and, hence, the monastery was an obvious place for them to gravitate towards. This same selectivity might account for other men being attracted to life in a military academy, a lighthouse or a submarine.

The significant point of this selective ritual theory is that by combining push and pull factors it underlines why *those* men were attracted to *that* sort of place. However, it needs to be made clear that the theory is also playing down the unique pull of the religious life because of its religious qualities. Rather, it is saying that those men were attracted to the monastic life largely because of their previous Christian experience and, hence, their somewhat latent awareness of the rituals of that life rather than its religious qualities. If their experiences had been different, then possibly they might have been attracted to some other setting.

A more detailed reading of this research account reveals a

number of tentative conclusions which were developed after analysis of approximately one third of the interview material. These conclusions, which were later borne out by the remaining interviews, are listed below.

(i) All men experienced what they defined as a major 'problem' in their previous work situations.

(ii) The dominant trend was that those problems centred around 'irregular hours', 'missed meals','constantly travelling and living out of a suitcase', and 'not knowing what was likely to happen next in the work situation'.

(iii) Several men professed to have been 'practising Christians' for many years.

(iv) Respondents claimed always to have had some sympathy for monastic life.

(v) The dominant response among the men was that they saw monastic life to be better because it 'is ordered', 'is planned so that you know what you should be doing at any one time' and 'is not boring even though you do the same thing every day'.

(vi) Most men explained the attraction of monastic life generally in terms of the above rather than spontaneously resorting to religious explanations, such as, 'I believe I was called to do this', 'a life of prayerful devotion is worthwhile', and 'I did it for God'.

(vii) Confidentially, some men confessed to doubting their own religious conviction at the same time as deriving great personal fulfilment from the ordered nature of monastic life.

The selective ritual theory springs directly from, or is based on, these conclusions. Repeated use of inverted commas indicates the words and concepts used by the participants in this study and it is those concepts which guide the development of the theory.

It is worth remembering here that all theories which are tested originally were constructed, so constructing a theory based on conclusions is really the reverse process of developing testable hypotheses from an existing theory. Although this account of research is brief, it provides enough detail to contrast with the first pattern and to act as a basis for a critical scrutiny.

A CRITICAL LOOK AT THIS EXAMPLE OF THEORY CON-
STRUCTION
In the above brief, critical look at theory testing research, the discussion was largely geared to demonstrating the signifi-cance of validity in developing hypotheses, and particularly in choosing indicators of sub concepts in those hypotheses. As we have seen, in theory construction where concepts are generated for the first time, the issue of validity does not exist. If 'the selective ritual theory', with its particular con-cepts, is an example of this type of theory construction, and let us assume it is, then what can we say about the methodo-logical weaknesses of this brief, hypothetical cameo of research? Although a more comprehensive account of the nature of analysis of research is the basis of the final chapter, two issues are worth identifying here to provide some illumi-nation of problems as they occur in the research context, albeit hypothetical. They are also worthy of comment be-cause they are generally neglected in the methodological literature.

The first issue is the use of quasi statistics (see Becker 1958; Rose 1982). Put simply, the use of quasi statistics in qualitative research involves the generation of propositions without numbers which aim to give a clear indication of proportions and/or the extent of any social event in relation to other social phenomena. For example, we might say that only a small minority of a class of students failed their exami-nation. We often do not need to know the precise size of the class or the actual percentage who failed. For the purposes at hand, we might assume that a small minority is up to 25%, which in a class of twenty students is another way of saying that as many as five students failed. By 'purposes at hand' I mean that it is not important to know whether one, a few or five failed. Just knowing that about that number and not, say, three quarters of the class failed is the important insight.

Quasi statistics should not be a device to obscure reality or encourage vagueness and, therefore, not all quasi statistics are equally sound. In our example of research in the monastery there are some vague quasi statistics which do not give a clear idea of what the researcher intended to say. Expressions such as 'as several put it', 'some' and 'typical' do not give a clear idea of the number or proportion of respondents involved. By contrast, other terms are more precise, such as 'all' and 'most'. The key point is that quasi statistics can and must be unambiguous. Whether as a good analyst of social research or as a researcher, it is therefore worth knowing some of the common vague statements found in the literature. These include:

- 'some'
- 'typical'
- 'a significant number'/'an insignificant number'
- 'a substantial proportion'
- 'a number worthy of mention'

The second issue is the relationship between the evidence and the theory being constructed. There are some crucial methodological points to grasp in this issue but, unfortunately, the available literature (e.g. see Becker 1958) renders them far too complex. It is helpful in simplifying this discussion to identify two types of concept and two types of relationship between the concept and the evidence. First, as we have already seen, there are participant's concepts and observer's concepts. As Figure 2.1 indicated, the existence of common patterns does not preclude the use of observer's concepts in theory construction research using participant observation. In fact, it is worth pointing out that in the hypothetical example above, the participants' concepts were the main focus in the conclusions, but the final name of the theory — the selective ritual theory — is provided by the observer or sociologist.

With reference to the relationship between the concepts and the evidence, there are two types:

(i) Dominant trend   When a researcher constructs a concept which is supported by qualitative evidence from most respondents and/or the most influential of their number, then we characterise the relationship between concept and evidence as a dominant trend. Research on a particular school or class room, for instance, may lead to the generation of the concept 'high achievers'. Not every person in the sample need provide evidence for this concept but, in terms of numbers and possibly the powerful actors in the situation, evidence supportive of 'high achievers' is the main pattern.

(ii) General quality   Concepts of this kind are supported by evidence from every case under investigation. Becker (1958), as indicated above, discusses this quality using the cumbersome term 'analytic induction'. Our same class of high achieving students could be regarded as 'gifted students' because every one provides sufficient evidence to warrant application of that concept (e.g. high IQ, plays a musical instrument and speaks another language).

By combining these comments about types of concept and types of relationship between concept and evidence, there are created four patterns (as Fig. 2.7 indicates). The insight from this relationship is that qualitative research should make it clear whose concepts are being used and, more to the point, whether they are dominant trends or based on all cases. Our example is not clear on this point. In some in-

Type of concept	Dominant trend	General quality
participant's	monastery provides ritual 'we, as a group, generally <u>need</u>'	all men had a '<u>problem</u>' in their former life
observer's	a class of '<u>high achievers</u>'	a class of '<u>gifted students</u>'

(concepts are indicated by underlining)

Figure 2.7   *Type of concepts and the relation between concepts and evidence*

stances 'all' respondents in the monastery are mentioned but in other places (and related to the problem of quasi statistics) it is not clear from expressions like 'as several put it', whether it refers to a concept which could be called a dominant trend. Again elsewhere, although it is obvious from the use of inverted commas that the participants' own concepts are being used, it is not clear in mentioning sympathy towards the monastic life whether this concept is a dominant trend or based on all cases.

Of course, there are other methodological problems in this mini example of qualitative research, such as the lack of discussion of the precise relationship the researcher had with respondents. Given it is difficult from this example to glean anything but a cursory understanding of participant observation, it is worthwhile making a more detailed comment on this method to acknowledge the main methodological points.

A CLOSER LOOK AT PARTICIPANT OBSERVATION

The main methodological point to stress is the importance of knowing the precise type of participant observation employed. Relevant literature discusses this point by stressing the significance of the 'role' of the researcher, which varies depending on the extent to which the researcher 'participates' in the setting being studied. 'Participates' means what it says. If a researcher wants to study, for example, the socialisation of nurses, then using the method of participant observation involves participating in the work settings of nurses. This would be very difficult if one were not actually a nurse, which opens up the significance of the researcher's role.

The role of the researcher using participant observation varies in terms of whether he/she is an 'insider' or an 'outsider'. By 'insider' I mean having a role in the eyes of other participants which is a part of the day to day routine of that social situation. Conversely, an 'outsider' participates as a 'researcher' and not in a role associated with that setting. If a researcher studying nurses in a hospital was also a nurse then, irrespective of whether other nurses knew they were being studied, we are able to say he/she is an 'insider' by virtue of being a nurse. Using degrees of participation (i.e. insider – outsider) in conjunction with participants' knowledge or ignorance of the identity of the researcher, we are able to clarify four discrete roles of researchers using this method and, hence, four types of participant observation.

Degree of participation	Type of role	Example
INSIDER	*Complete participant* — is a legitimate participant but is not known to be a researcher by other participants.	Clandestine study by a nurse of day to day routines in a hospital.
	Participant-as-observer — is a legitimate participant but is known to be a researcher by other participants.	Researcher who obtains a job as a warder in a prison to study prison culture.
OUTSIDER	*Observer-as-participant* — participates in routine activities but is not a legitimate participant and, therefore, is known to be a researcher.	Sociologist who studies the nature of religious life by living in a monastery and attending all activities.
	Observer — does not participate in routine activities but observes activities 'at a distance' but with full knowledge of those being studied. Researcher is a participant only in this weak sense.	Sociologist who studies factory production by observing all shop floor activities from an observation post nearby.

Figure 2.8 *Types of participant observation*

This picture is elaborated in Figure 2.8.

The point of this brief discussion of participant observation is not to convey the method but to provide a background for understanding the methodological problems associated with its use. As indicated, the major issue involves knowing the type of participant observation employed. Problems arise when researchers do not make clear what degree of participation they had. If, for example, you were reading an account of a study of unions in which a sociologist participated in the day to day routines of union officials, it is crucial to know whether the sociologist was a complete participant or a participant-as-observer. It is crucial because this distinction might explain the absence of evidence surrounding the rationale for organisers' decision making. If the sociologist had been a complete participant, then the nature of the method could explain gaps in the evidence. This is because full participants in social settings (insiders) can not easily ask outsiders' questions. A nurse doing a study as a complete participant would find it very difficult to ask colleagues 'why is working to a routine important in this hospital ward?' Such questions are strange coming from a colleague because they are outside the understandings taken for granted in that situation. However, these sorts of questions are not strange if asked by participants who are known to be researchers. Therefore, if our sociologist was posing as a union official, that is, a complete participant, then this could explain the gap in important evidence. However, if that role had been participant-as-observer, the desired evidence would have been, in principle, more accessible, thus making its absence more of a problem. This problem is obviously compounded when researchers themselves do not understand the implications of their differing degrees of participation and, hence, their different roles in the settings they study.

Knowing the precise role of the researcher is also crucial (for both reader and researcher) because different roles are associated with different ways of perceiving the situation. At a theoretical level, this point is closely related to the discussion of theory dependence in the previous chapter. At an empirical level, it is well illustrated by Asher's (1986) study of a boy's juvenile prison. Asher began the study by attending the prison on a regular basis and interviewing and observing day to day practices (an observer-as-participant). Later he obtained employment in the institution as a warder and was then able to observe the situation from a different vantage point (a participant-as-observer). The instructive point for our purposes is that Asher describes his change of outlook in his change of role. Whereas he began the study as a somewhat sympathetic outsider concerned for the welfare of juvenile offenders, as a warder he was aware of becoming less sympathetic and more matter of fact in approaching their predicament.

Of course, there is a lot more that could be said about participant observation but this brief discussion is only intended to raise obvious methodological issues. Interested students will find texts such as Filstead (1971) and McCall and Simmons (1969) helpful.

To conclude this chapter, it is worthwhile using the above discussion, especially the distinction between theory testing and theory construction research, to see to what extent it is a realistic characterisation of social research.

Research as both theory testing and theory construction

In reality, the distinction between theory testing and theory construction research is more a statement of broad trends rather than firm categories. That is, although social research inclines towards one type or the other, few instances are exclusively of one type. To this point, treating theory testing and theory construction research separately in their 'pure' form is important for understanding more clearly the assumptions and steps associated with each type and for understanding the actual task of doing social research. On the basis of these comments it is evident that most actual re-

search has elements of both theory testing and theory construction. This is brought to light by first briefly examining
different characterisations of research activity and then looking more specifically at some familiar sociological studies.

The scientific method is often portrayed in textbooks as
the characterisation of research activity in a variety of fields.
On closer inspection, this method is anything but uniform.
In some instances, research is a four stage process which
concludes with a theory.

1 Hypothesis
2 Collect and record facts of observation
3 Classification
4 Generalisation from facts

Others, by contrast, point to a different path in which the
starting point is the theory.

1 Theory
2 Hypothesis
3 Collect data
4 Principle formation or generalisation

If this were another way of presenting theory construction
and theory testing in another guise, then there would be little
to comment on. However, this picture becomes more complex. Scientific method is also viewed as a process of a
different kind.

1 Having an idea
2 Collecting data
3 Forming hypotheses
4 Testing hypotheses
5 Relating findings to broader issues (see Hoult 1979: 93)

Wallace (1971) departs from the straight line view of the
scientific method and characterises it as a circle in which
several 'circuts' of the four stages are possible and, in fact,
desirable since research proceeds 'through one spiralling cy-
cle around the diagram after another, as each component is
improved in its turn' (1971: ix–x). In Wallace's circle, research could start with a theory and end up with a different
theory (see Fig. 2.9). Wallace's notion of repeated spirals is

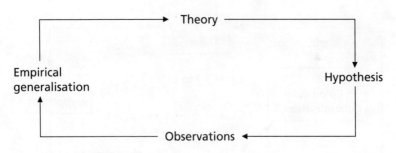

Figure 2.9 *Wallace's model of the research process*

not accurately conveyed by his own diagram. Without wishing to complicate the process of research, a more realistic picture is conveyed by Figure 2.10, which is a modification of Wallace's diagram. Steps A to L demonstrate that research is actually a process of continually formulating, testing and modifying theories.

The principle of research being both theory testing and theory construction is conveyed by our more prominent, medical analogy. When a doctor thinks you have hepatitis and tests that theory only to find that it is not the case, another diagnosis usually follows given the extent of test results at hand. Here theory testing is followed by theory construction. On the other hand, if the doctor did not know why you were ill and did a wide range of tests to find out, the results may not have produced a diagnosis but may have provided enough evidence to narrow the problem down to one or two explanations, which could be tested in turn. Here theory construction is followed by theory testing.

Social science research mirrors this medical analogy. The two pieces of research which are analysed in the next chapter were chosen because each is as close as one will get to having 'pure' theory testing and theory construction research. Nevertheless, we find in both examples elements of both types of research, albeit implicit.

In conclusion, it is important to stress the methodological value of understanding the principles of both types of re-

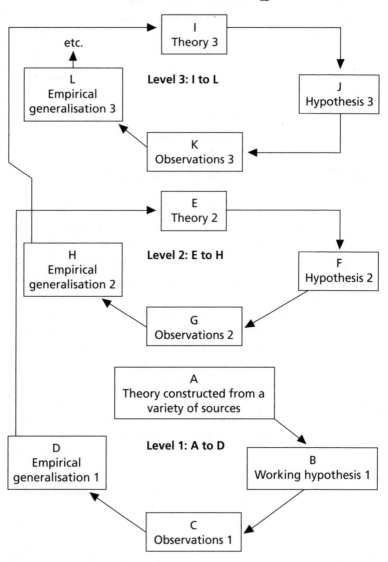

Figure 2.10 *Modification of Wallace's model of the re-search process*

search in their 'pure' form. The fact that all social research is more or less both theory testing and theory construction means that it is more competently analysed by understanding those principles. It is analysis of social research which is the focus of the next chapter.

3
The Nature of the Analysis of Social Research

'Analysis' is one of those terms students frequently encounter in social science courses. Along with other terms, such as 'abstract', 'causality' and 'theory', 'analysis' is often used but just as often poorly understood. The best way of understanding this important term is to regard it as a process in which the *methodological principles* of research are applied to *specific pieces* of research. In other words, we can view analysis as the systematic and critical scrutiny of assumptions behind the various parts of a piece of research and of their implementation. Comparing this to our definition of methodology — 'the systematic scrutiny of what researchers do and why they do it' — we have a statement of particular practice alongside of a general principle.

Any discussion which aims to equip students with analytic skills should have something instructive to say about the practical steps involved in doing analysis. This short chapter addresses this task. It elaborates the point that 'critical scrutiny' means subjecting all aspects of the planning and execution of research to questions derived from an understanding of the issues discussed in Chapters 1 and 2. By 'systematic' I mean having a coherent plan or strategy for addressing those questions. The outline in Chapter 2 of two common patterns of research, and the discussion of theory dependence in Chapter 1, clarify what is meant by research having 'assumptions' behind its various 'steps'.

The strategy for analysis outlined below is based on the distinction between theory testing and theory construction research. It cannot be emphasised too strongly that this distinction is for our benefit as methodologists and is not meant to be a statement of two rigid categories of social research. This point was defended in Chapter 2 with the demonstration that although social research tends either towards theory testing or theory construction it also often has elements of both approaches. The purpose of having a strategy of analysis based on these approaches is to enable the student analysing a piece of research to see to what extent it contains elements of each approach. This strengthens analysis because these approaches to research, although generally co-existing, are based on different assumptions and involve different steps in their implementation.

In principle, the difference between theory testing and theory construction is emphasised by the different questions asked of each in a strategy for analysis, which is presented in Figures 3.1 and 3.2. This strategy assumes that most research fits into either of the two patterns discussed in Chapter 2. Its use involves addressing each of the questions surrounding the various steps of the research. Obviously, because of the many combinations of research which are possible (e.g. theory testing research which adopts a qualitative approach to evidence and uses participant observation and observer's concepts) this strategy for analysis will not exactly fit all variations. Depending on those combinations, modifications to the strategy will have to be made whereby questions are 'borrowed' from the theory testing side and vice-versa. However, a clear understanding of methodology, which hopefully this book provides, will enable straightforward modifications to be made.

In the section which follows, this strategy is applied to two pieces of social research — the first, predominantly theory testing, fitting pattern 1; the second, theory construction, fitting pattern 2.

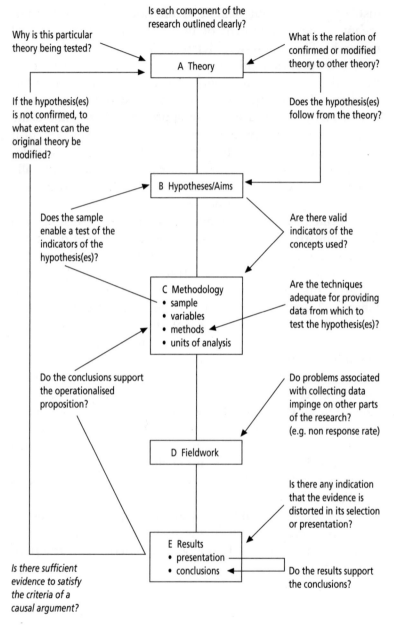

Figure 3.1 *A guide for analysis of theory testing research*

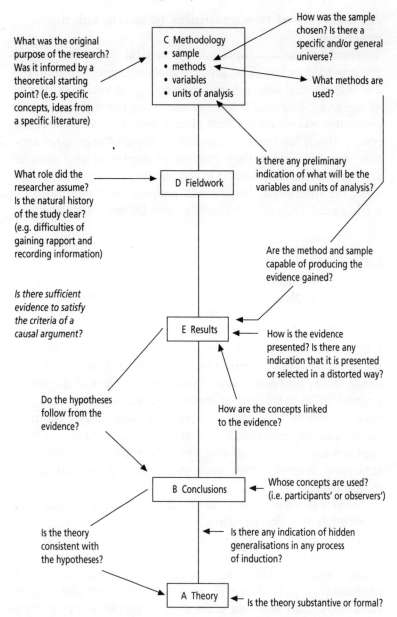

What was the original purpose of the research? Was it informed by a theoretical starting point? (e.g. specific concepts, ideas from a specific literature)

C Methodology
• sample
• methods
• variables
• units of analysis

How was the sample chosen? Is there a specific and/or general universe?

What methods are used?

What role did the researcher assume? Is the natural history of the study clear? (e.g. difficulties of gaining rapport and recording information)

D Fieldwork

Is there any preliminary indication of what will be the variables and units of analysis?

Are the method and sample capable of producing the evidence gained?

Is there sufficient evidence to satisfy the criteria of a causal argument?

E Results

How is the evidence presented? Is there any indication that it is presented or selected in a distorted way?

Do the hypotheses follow from the evidence?

How are the concepts linked to the evidence?

B Conclusions

Whose concepts are used? (i.e. participants' or observers')

Is the theory consistent with the hypotheses?

Is there any indication of hidden generalisations in any process of induction?

A Theory

Is the theory substantive or formal?

Figure 3.2 *A guide for analysis of theory construction research*

An analysis of two examples of social science research

To reinforce the development of analytical skills two analyses are provided below. The articles analysed represent patterns 1 and 2 of social research and, moreover, are probably typical of the most extreme instances of theory testing and theory construction one encounters. These analyses can be usefully read without having any acquaintance with the original articles simply because they provide examples of the sorts of answers to questions asked in the strategy for analysis. However, the interested student will gain considerably more by having read Dowse and Hughes' and Birksted's articles.

DOWSE AND HUGHES' 'GIRLS, BOYS AND POLITICS'
Dowse and Hughes' (1971; see also Rose 1982: 231–243) attempt to explain the different rates of participation of males and females in politics. Why do women vote less, know less about and have less interest in politics, participate less in political parties and think more conservatively? The authors try to address this question by testing the role model theory which holds that political socialisation is a facet of the wider process of socialisation of males and females into their respective gender based social roles. This theory, they claim, is an alternative explanation to the structural theory which explains females' lack of participation in politics in terms of structural impediments, such as child rearing and home maintenance.

From the role model theory the authors generate two hypotheses for direct testing.

(i) 'Political sex differences apparent in childhood will increase with age as the roles become more clearly defined'.

(ii) 'Since middle class girls are better educated than working class girls, they will consistently be more like middle class boys than working class girls resemble working class boys'.

The first clearly derives from role model theory. However,

there is a problem with the derivation of the second because its confirmation would not necessarily result from 'better education', which is the authors' assumption. We know enough from other research in the sociology of education to recognise the often spurious role of education, which can act as a proxy for the more influential role of family background. Notwithstanding this logical objection, it is surprising that the authors did not present more and simpler hypotheses. Confirmation of a more straightforward proposition, such as 'middle class girls resemble middle class boys rather than working class girls', would suggest that role modelling does not take place along the rigid gender lines assumed by the theory, and that other factors such as class background also play a role. Also, one can imagine additional hypotheses to strengthen the test of the theory. If assessing the extent to which education offsets the role of family is important, then something like 'boarding school girls have higher political knowledge than day school girls in the same school' would be less problematical than the second hypothesis. This is because boarding school girls could be viewed as the exemplars of the maximum role of education and the minimum role of family in the process of socialisation. However, on a logical point, the authors are correct in saying that if the hypotheses are confirmed, then there is a 'possibility' of the theory explaining the difference. This is because confirmation of the hypotheses does not guarantee the truth of the theory, although it is not clear that the problem of 'affirming the consequent' is the reason for the authors' caution.

There are a couple of problems in the operationalisation stage of this research. First, although indicators of 'age', 'sex' and, possibly, 'party choice' and 'media exposure' raise few difficulties, those for 'school type' or 'education', 'class' and 'political sex differences' are more problematical. Grammar and secondary modern schools may represent those types of education catering to most students in the United Kingdom, but the choice of particular schools ignores co-educational schools which, in terms of the socialising role of education,

important. Additionally, in the schools chosen it is
r that there is a range of education in terms of
'higher' and 'more' — terms frequently employed by
the authors. 'Class' has similar problems. No hint is given as
to which theoretical tradition that concept derives from and,
notwithstanding the previous point, a simple manual – non
manual categorisation of occupations as the basis of class is
inadequate. For instance, although it is stated that parents'
occupations are the indicators of class, there is no suggestion
as to how children with parents from different classes might
be categorised. Some of the indicators of 'political sex differences' also have difficulties. We are told that the 'most clear
cut difference' emerged from answers to two dozen questions
testing political knowledge. However, based on the examples
given (which were at the level of asking children to name the
local member of parliament and provide the names of the
two houses of parliament) those questions could arguably be
regarded as testing general rather than political knowledge.

A second type of problem stems from sole reliance on one
method — the questionnaire. Specifically, the likelihood of
untruthfulness and game playing among schoolchildren in
completing questionnaires is high. It would appear that the
authors had a 100% response rate in administering their
questionnaire. If so, this needs to be stated and then it only
raises further questions about the likelihood of game playing.
Without some other type of corroborative evidence, such as
interviews with teachers, it is difficult to regard those particular questions as good indicators of the concepts they were
designed to measure.

Although the authors state that the hypotheses were not
confirmed by the data, it is important to understand the
reasoning by which they arrive at this main conclusion. An
examination of three sub conclusions reveals the inadequacy
of evidence for them. First, the claim that the first hypothesis
is weakly confirmed in secondary modern schools. At face
value, the evidence in their Figure 16.1 seems to support this
conclusion. However, on closer examination we find not

numbers but percentages. We know that around 50% of 11–12 year old grammar boys are high scorers, but how many? Of a total of 146 grammar boys, it could be the case that the 11–12 year olds constitute, say, only ten boys. That would mean five high scorers in this category, a number far too small from which to derive accurate inferences. Another problem with this figure is that we do not know what a high score is. Although the sample is divided into tertiles, we do not know, for example, whether the middle third are only a few percentage points below the high scorers. This sort of information is important because proximity of scores in each tertile would weaken claims about the significance of high scorers.

Second, the authors claim that the second hypothesis is partly confirmed by 'the following evidence' and then proceed to describe their interpretation of evidence not included in the article. This is not a substitute for evidence but, more important, they do not adequately incorporate the role of age in that evidence. If socialisation is the key process in the explanation of political sex differences, then the use of age is the only way one can demonstrate more or less socialisation into gender specific roles.

Finally, it is also claimed that 'taking the spread of political knowledge across the whole sample, the hypothesis is confirmed'. But again the key evidence for this conclusion, their Table 16.1, does not incorporate age. This is crucial because, as noted earlier, 'better education' is viewed in terms of 'higher' and 'more' education. Generally, it is important to note the authors' disregard for the concept of age, with only two figures and one table including it.

Dowse and Hughes use their conclusions to question the assumption of socialisation theory that generations replicate themselves. Further, they suggest that they are forced to conclude one of two things: that generations are not politically replicated on the basis of childhood socialisation 'or' that structural factors are more important than socialisation theory suggests. It is difficult to see why they say 'or', 'because' would seem to make more sense.

One final point in this analysis is that the authors do not touch on an important aspect of the wider body of sociological theory, which would appear obvious in this study. To conclude that socialisation theory overstresses the role of attitudes, and to juxtapose this theory, with structural theory, immediately suggests the issue of the role of ideas in the social world. This should prompt some mention of theorists such as Weber and Marx and schools of thought such as idealism and materialism.

BIRKSTED'S 'SCHOOL PERFORMANCE VIEWED FROM THE BOYS'

The purpose of Birksted's article (1976; see also Rose 1982: 265–75) is clearly stated in the opening paragraphs: to clarify 'what "school" meant to a selected number of adolescents'. In this study the idea of exploring the meaning of 'school' entails understanding adolescents' rather than school authorities' definitions of the situation. This aim springs from Birksted's familiarity with the sociology of education, especially that concerned with success and failure in school. Most of this literature, according to Birksted, is either comparative (comparing school values and social class values) or interactionist (focusing on classroom processes which stress the role of the teacher in students' eventual success or failure). Both bodies of literature define success and failure in the schools' own terms, that is, using school related definitions of the situation. This claim provides the rationale for Birksted's concern with locating students' own understanding of their situation; hence the title of the article and the statement of the tentative or working assumption that it is the boys' choices and strategies which impinge on success and failure.

At face value Birksted's article is a straightforward instance of theory construction research. However, it actually has elements of both theory testing and theory construction. The theory construction is explicit. More implicit is Birksted's testing of certain ideas from the sociology of education. That is, by deriving his counter position from that literature, Birksted proceeds, albeit implicitly, to test it with his own research. Put differently, if his evidence eventually showed that the boys' own definition of the situation was not all that influential, it may indicate that school oriented theories in the sociology of education are more credible than initially supposed.

The *sample* was chosen in the 'catchment area' of a comprehensive school. However, Birksted provides no indication of why that area and school were chosen. Although, in terms of the outcome of the research, the reasons for choosing that particular school are not critical, it is important for researchers to provide some hint as to how such choices are made. This is important because many convenience samples are made possible through friendship networks (e.g. Becker's well known article 'Becoming a marijuana user') or residential and/or work proximity (e.g. Goldthorpe *et al The Affluent Worker*). Knowing this relationship between research and the eventual choice of sample helps to focus on the researcher's entree and rapport with those being studied, especially in participant observation research. In Birksted's article, all we know is that within the catchment area the author regularly attended a youth and community centre for two months and then successfully approached the local school where the boys attended. The eventual sample was an atypical group of eight boys with emphasis placed on six. These boys were a friendship group and were viewed somewhat negatively by teachers at the school.

As far as *methods* are concerned, it is clear from the article that participant observation was used. However, it is not completely clear what degree of participation was involved, especially in the school phase of the study. It can be inferred that he was an observer-as-participant in the youth and community centre, for he indicates that the boys at the centre knew he was a sociology research student writing a book and, although not stated, it is obvious that he was considerably older than the boys he mixed with. This information is important because it bears on the progress of the study, especially the difficulty of gaining entree and rapport with those being studied.

Although Birksted's role in the youth and community centre was observer-as-participant, his role in the school is not so apparent. At first glance it is reasonable to think that he entered the school as a participant (i.e. as a teacher) but this role was unlikely as he states that he knew no school staff and was initially not accepted by them. Knowing the role of the researcher is crucial because it influences the progress of the study, especially the reactions of participants, which in turn affects the quality of the data. We know, for instance, that Birksted's reception at the youth and community centre was apparently straightforward, but the initial non-acceptance of Birksted by teachers and the growth of his legitimacy as he gained acceptance by the boys point to a big question mark surrounding his role, that is, what did he actually do in the school phase of the research?

Birksted's closing references to the significance of 'self-definition', 'perception of school' and 'social environment' indicate that his earlier mention of 'strategies and choices','children's views of themselves' and 'social environment' were an indication of the sorts of variables he anticipated encountering. Similarly, it is obvious from his early description of his orientation to the research that individual students' accounts will be the units of analysis.

In terms of the progress of the study, one aspect is clear — the method of recording information. Birksted clearly states on a couple of occasions that he used a tape recorder in the course of his research. The method would generally appear to be adequate in producing the evidence Birksted presents. We know he spent two months with the boys at the youth and community centre, possibly a period of months in the school, and then a greater part of the summer holidays in close contact with them. In this particular study the sample is not problematical as it is not a probability sample and, hence, wider generalisations are not made.

It would appear that there are at least six hypotheses or conclusions generated from the data. Unlike hypotheses to be tested with data, these are not clearly signalled and have to be extracted from the text. Also, given that the concepts employed are not of an abstract nature but spring from the participants' own definition of the situation, the hypotheses appear commonsensical and possibly trivial. However, their consideration is important in the overall analysis of Birksted because they do not emerge from the mouths of the boys. In other words, the hypotheses are not raw data. This is evident when they are examined in isolation.

(i) School breaks are not gaps between classes but classes are interruptions to the gathering.

(ii) No distinction is made between term time and holiday time.

(iii) Work is not exemplified by or identified with school.

(iv) School occupies time.

(v) To be on holiday is to go away.

(vi) The utility of school is related to future jobs.

Turning to the evidence, its presentation involves using summary statements of what the boys said. For example, 'they said they enjoyed the trip and told me many stories . . .', and extracts of tape-recorded interviews. Such 'second hand' accounts make it difficult to assess whether all hypotheses follow from the evidence. Only the fifth hypothesis and, to a lesser extent, the sixth are supported by what could be regarded as the actual words of the boys. In this sort of situation we simply have to accept Birksted's claims about evidence at face value.

Associated with this problem of the presentation of evidence is the problem of the vagueness of the concept – evidence link. Although we know that Birksted uses participants' concepts rather than generating his own observer concepts, we do not know whether his conclusions are supported by every case or whether they indicate the main trends among the boys. The validity of concepts does not arise in this study simply because, as participants' concepts, they are embedded in the evidence. However, this question could apply where the concepts generated derive from a known body of theory, such as Marx's notion of 'class'. Given the frequent use of existing concepts in theory construction research, scrutiny of validity is important only in those cases.

Concerning the construction of theory, we see in Birksted's closing comments an attempt to present an explanatory, albeit brief, theory which accounts for the situation he found in the school. Specifically, he proposes that the boys are not anti-school but a-school. School is not an organising principle in their lives. To assess whether this theory is consistent with the hypotheses, all one need do is assume that the theory is to be tested and to ask whether one could derive or deduce the hypotheses from the theory. That is, if the theory is true, then would the hypotheses follow? In Birksted's case, the answer would appear to be 'yes'. Finally, this limited theory is a substantive theory in that it applies only to the substantive area of education. If, for instance, Birksted had focused on a large random sample of boys, his theory would have been formal if it had proposed, say, that their behaviour was a result of lack of social integration in all their social environments. Such a theory does not apply nor is it confined to one substantive area.

As a final comment, Birksted's article (which is typical of a pattern of research characterised by theory construction, qualitative assumptions about evidence, the use of participant observation and participants' concepts) achieves only a part of its original aim. It is successful in unveiling the nature of the boys' definition of the situation in the school, but it stops short in determining whether and to what extent this is influential in shaping behaviour. The latter shortcoming possibly springs from the absence of consideration of the important question of whether beliefs (including definitions of the situation) are ever determinants of behaviour.

These brief analyses are provided to demonstrate the strategy of analysis outlined earlier. Good analysis, which involves systematically applying the principles of methodology, is essentially a question answering exercise, that is, addressing the questions in Figures 3.1 and 3.2. However, one word of caution is needed. It is not always possible to derive answers to all questions when applying this strategy. These questions are an inclusive list and some may not be appropriate in some instances of social research. On the other hand, gaps in some works, which prevent our answering specific questions, may be a methodological weakness. It is up to the student-as-methodologist to discern the difference.

Glossary of Important Terms

This glossary defines and annotates some of the more important terms used in the text. It provides a quick, concise comment on those terms and, where appropriate, further reading.

Abstraction   This term refers to the process of selection from the phenomena we study, those traits which capture the character of what we want to describe and which form the basis of further classification. Such description and classification results in the generation of more or less abstract concepts. For example, a term such as 'high achievers' which may stem from studying levels of motivation among school children is generated by giving significance to those specific traits among children which the researcher is initially interested in. The word 'specific' is important because not all traits of children would be used in generating the notion of 'high achiever'. This term could then be used for widespread classification of children's levels of motivation.

Analysis   One difficulty in defining 'analysis' is that it means different things to different researchers in a variety of disciplines. However, we can abstract (see 'abstraction') some common elements to suggest that analysis is a process in which the constituent parts of that which is being analysed are identified and their relations established with the aim of understanding how the whole entity and/or its parts are constituted and/or function. This definition would cover, for example, 'analysis' of some unknown substance in a forensic laboratory and what happens when scholars critically scrutinise a research paper or book.

Concepts, conceptual   Concepts are 'images of reality' (Rose 1982: 305) and are used not only in the sciences but also in everyday life. 'Cup', 'war', 'transport' and 'love' are all concepts but are at different levels of abstraction (see 'abstraction'). 'Concept' and 'conceptual framework' are unnecessarily confusing for social science students probably because of the assumption that 'concepts' belong to a more exclusive realm which is difficult to apprehend. If there is any difficulty, then it is more likely to be in understanding the notion of 'abstraction' rather than in grasping the nature of a 'concept' (see Rose 1982: 34ff.; Mitchell 1968: 37).

Empirical   Although 'empirical' has several meanings it should not be confused with 'empiricism', which is a derogatory term characterising research without theoretical orientation. 'Empirical' is a neutral term often used to describe research which gathers new evidence in contrast to research which relies on secondary sources, that is, 'library research'. This use of the term is unsatisfactory because a number of disciplines rely heavily on library sources for evidence (e.g. history) and it does not make sense to say they are not empirical if the term is to have anything to do with the role of evidence in research. For a more extended discussion, see Mitchell (1968: 66–67).

Explanation   see 'theory'

Independent variable, dependent variable, intervening variable   In a causal relationship between two or more variables, the independent variable (A) is that which influences another variable but which is not influenced itself. The dependent variable (C) is the 'end product' or that which is caused. A variable which influences another variable and is also influenced by an independent variable is known as an intervening variable (B). As the discussion in the text indicates, saying that an independent variable is not influenced is purely for the purposes at hand. In reality, nothing is uncaused. See also 'variable'.

[A] ⟶ [B] ⟶ [C]

Indicator   Indicators are used to test the presence of certain concepts which are not directly testable in the material world. The question on many forms and questionnaires 'what is your date of birth?' is an indicator of the concept 'age'. It indicates age, which is not directly observable. Rose (1982: 309) notes that an 'indicator is a variable; the separate terms are maintained because "indicator" makes it clear that a "concept" is being measured'. This is clear when questionnaire items are considered. Responses to those items, or questions, vary but at the same time are often indicators of certain concepts in the theory being tested.

Median, cf. mean, mode   These terms occur frequently in the social science literature. The *mean* is what we generally understand by the term 'average', that is, the sum of all the values divided by the number of values. The *median* is the mid point in a range of values. The *mode* is the most numerous or represented category or value in a range. In the following range of individuals' heights, the mean is 160.5cm, the median is 180cm, and the mode is 185cm: 100cm, 120cm, 140cm, 160cm, 180cm, 185cm, 185cm, 185cm, 190cm.

Methodology   In the text, methodology is defined as 'the systematic scrutiny of what researchers do and why they do it', which is another way of saying that methodology is the study of the logical or philosophical basis of any discipline. Unfortunately, this term has been used loosely, so that in some circumstances it refers only to the study of methods in a discipline.

Operationalisation   This is the process of deciding what will count as evidence for the concepts contained in a theory. Making decisions about evidence also entails decisions about the method(s) of obtaining it.

Questionnaire   The questionnaire is a more complex tool than the short discussion in the text might indicate. Apart from understanding the more obvious points, such as when to use a particular type of questionnaire (e.g. mailed or interviewer administered; fixed choice or open-ended questions), there are technical issues surrounding wording and layout (e.g. see Selltiz *et al.* 1976; Oppenheim 1966). Some indication of the subtle nature of wording is covered in the text. For a more detailed discussion, especially in relation to the amount of information given in questions used in polling, see Goot (1985).

Reliability The extent to which any research method will consistently give the same results when administered under the same conditions is a measure of its reliability. The everyday sense of reliability is useful in understanding how the term is applied to social research, because when we say a thermometer or a clock is reliable we are using the term in exactly the same way. Reliability should not be confused with validity (see 'validity').

Sampling, sample The selection of units for study in any research is a sampling process. This is because it is generally impossible to study every case in a particular frame of reference. Common instances of sampling include pollsters generating population samples and doctors taking a sample of blood for certain tests. Only in certain research, such as the study of cooperation in a football team, is the whole population or number of things being studied called the sample. Probability sampling aims to provide a representative cross section of a particular population, or whatever is being studied, so that generalisations can be made about that population. In principle, a representative sample of people is obtained from random selection, as in a lottery. In practice, there is however the problem of non response, that is, those individuals who, for whatever reason, refuse to be interviewed or complete a questionnaire. Social scientists also use other types of population samples. Convenience samples, for example, are those samples generated, as the name suggests, at the convenience of the researcher. It may be a town near the researcher's place of residence, a number of people who live in the same apartment building, or your own family or colleagues. If this sort of sampling is employed because a representative sample was not possible, then there

are problems if generalisations are made to the wider population of what is being studied. However, there are occasions
when the sample required is not representative. Goldthorpe
et al.'s The Affluent Worker was a 'critical test' sample. Their
study examined the population of Luton, England, because
they believed it was among those people that one would be
most likely to see signs of the working class becoming more
middle class. For a concise discussion of sampling, see Rose
(1982: chapter 4).

Scientific method   This method is often cited in the
literature of many disciplines as the preferred method of
gathering evidence and formulating new insights. It is the
preferred approach because it is uncritically regarded as a
protection against the researcher's own biases entering the
research process. As is evident in the text, the scientific
method is really a mode of proceeding with the stages of
research. There is nothing intrinsic to those stages which acts
as a foil against unwanted bias. Hempel (1966) and Chalmers
(1982) together are very useful further reading.

Theory   'Theory' is, as Mitchell (1968: 211) notes, 'one
of the most misused and misleading terms in the vocabulary
of the social scientist'. In the text, an attempt is made to give
more precision and understanding to this term. If we regard
'theory' as the attempt to account for a given phenomenon,
that is, to show what, how and/or why it is, then it can be
equated with 'explanation'. As the terms 'what', 'how' and
'why' imply, explanation of social events is a more-or-less
phenomenon illustrated in the text by the discussion of causal
theory, laws, models and so on.

Theory dependence, theory ladenness   This term is
often used in an imprecise and unclear way. It refers to the
influence of certain, often unstated, assumptions on the research process. For a more detailed and clear discussion of
one aspect of theory dependence — the problem of induction
— see Chalmers (1982).

Unit of analysis   Rose (1982: 55ff.) notes that in much
sociological research the unit of analysis is 'the individual

person'. However, I would prefer to use this term to refer to that which is actually analysed in a research project. If, for example, the only method used in a research project is a questionnaire, then the units of analysis would be the actual responses to each of the questions contained in the questionnaire. Obviously such responses are those of each 'individual person', but, on a technical point, in this example the researcher would not actually analyse individuals but what they say. 'Units of analysis' should not be confused with 'units of study' (see 'sampling'), which are the units contained in the theory or theoretical framework. Individuals are often the units of study, but other units include schools, classes, organisations and groups.

Validity, valid   When one proposition follows from or is logically derived from another, then it is valid. This quality we refer to as validity. Valid indicators of concepts, therefore, are those which are thought to follow from or are logically derived from a theory. It is thought that by using those indicators, a researcher would be really getting at what he/she intended to measure at the theoretical level. 'Thought' implies the difficulty of establishing validity. There are no exact tests to guarantee that all indicators are valid. However, Rose (1982: 42) discusses procedures which can reinforce a researcher's confidence of having validity.

Variable   A variable is an identifiable characteristic which varies in a research setting. Rose (1982: 309) views variables as characteristics which vary between individuals in a sample, but this is a little restrictive. In research which uses questionnaires, the variables are the questions themselves to which individuals respond (see 'indicator'). However, in other research where the units of analysis (see 'units of analysis') are, for example, written accounts in documents, the variables could be the presence or absence of any discussion of particular issues; the amount of space given over to such discussion; or even the frequency of grammatical errors.

References

Almack, John C. (1930) *Research and Thesis Writing*, New York: Houghton Mifflin.

Asher, Geoff. (1986) *Custody and Control*, Sydney: Allen & Unwin.

Becker, H. S. (1958) 'Problems of inference and proof in participant observation', *American Sociological Review* 23: 652–60.

Birksted, Ian K. (1976) 'School performance viewed from the boys', *Sociological Review* 24: 63–77.

Brown, Robert (1963) *Explanation in Social Science*, London: Routledge & Kegan Paul.

Butler, D. and Kitzinger, U. W. (1976) *The 1975 Referendum*, London: Macmillan.

Chalmers, A. F. (1982) *What is This Thing Called Science?*, 2nd edition, St. Lucia: University of Queensland Press.

Coser, Rose Laub (1976) 'Suicide and the relational system: a case study in a mental hospital', *Journal of Health and Social Behavior* 17 (Dec.): 318–27.

Dowse, Robert E. and Hughes, John A. (1971) 'Girls, boys and politics', *British Journal of Sociology* 22: 53–67.

Feyerabend, P. K. (1975) *Against Method: Outline of an Anarchistic Theory of Knowledge*, London: New Left Books.

Filstead, William J. (1971) *Qualitative Methodology: First Hand Involvement With the Social World*, Chicago: Mackham.

Gibbs, Jack (1972) *Sociological Theory Construction*, Hinsdale, Ill.: The Dryden Press.

Goot, Murray (1985) 'Public opinion and the public opinion polls' in A. Markus and M. C. Ricklefs (eds) *Surrender Australia?*, Sydney: George Allen & Unwin.

Hempel, Carl G. (1966) *Philosophy of Natural Science*, Englewood Cliffs, N.J.

Hirst, Paul Q. (1975) *Durkheim, Bernard and Epistemology*, London: Routledge & Kegan Paul.

———— (1976) *Social Evolution and Sociological Categories*, London: George Allen & Unwin.

Hoult, Thomas Ford (1979) *Sociology For a New Day*, 2nd edition, New York: Random House.

Humphreys, Laud (1971) *Tea Room Trade: Impersonal Sex in Public Places*, Chicago: Aldine.

Jones, Gareth Stedman (1977) 'History: the poverty of empiricism' in Blackburn (ed), *Ideology in Social Science*, Glasgow: Fontana-Collins.

Kuhn, T. S. (1970) *The Structure of Scientific Revolutions*, Chicago: Chicago University Press.

Labovitz, Sanford and Hagedorn, Robert (1971) *Introduction to Social Research*, New York: McGraw Hill.

Lewins, Frank (1988) *Writing a Thesis: A Guide to Its Nature and Organisation*, Canberra: Faculty of Arts, ANU.

McCall, G. J. and Simmons, J. L. (1969) *Issues in Participant Observation*, Reading, Mass.: Addison-Wesley.

Mitchell, G. D. ed. (1968) *A Dictionary of Sociology*, London: Routledge & Kegan Paul.

Ollman, Bertell (1986) 'Introduction' in Ollman and Vernoff (eds), *Left Academy: Marxist Scholarship on American Campuses 3*, New York: Praeger.

Oppenheim, A. N. (1966) *Questionnaire Design and Attitude Measurement*, London: Heinemann.

Popper, K. R. (1968) *The Logic of Scientific Discovery*, London: Hutchinson.

_____ (1972) *Objective Knowledge*, Oxford: Oxford University Press.

Rose, Gerry (1982) *Deciphering Sociological Research*, London: Macmillan.

Rummel, Francis J. (1964) *An Introduction to Research Procedures in Education*, 2nd edition, New York: Harper and Row.

Salmon, Wesley C. (1963) Logic, Englewood Cliffs, N.J.: Prentice Hall.

Selltiz, C. *et al.* (1976) *Research Methods in Social Relations*, New York: Holt Rinehart & Winston.

Stinchcombe, Arthur L. (1968) *Constructing Social Theories*, New York: Harcourt Brace & World Inc.

Swanson, Guy (1967) *Religion and Regime: A Sociological Account of the Reformation*, Ann Arbor, Michigan: University of Michigan Press.

Wallace, Walter (1971) *Sociological Theory*, London: Heinemann.

Willer, Judith (1971) *The Social Determination of Knowledge*, Englewood Cliffs, N.J.: Prentice Hall Inc.

_____ and Willer, David (1973) *Systematic Empiricism: Critique of a Pseudoscience*, Englewood Cliffs, N.J.: Prentice Hall Inc.

Youngson, A. J. (1979) *The Scientific Revolution in Victorian Medicine*, Canberra: Australian National University Press.

Index